BIG BOWL™

NOODLES AND RICE

BIG BOWL™

NOODLES AND RICE

FRESH ASIAN COOKING FROM THE RENOWNED RESTAURANT

BRUCE COST

with CHEF MATT McMILLIN

PHOTOGRAPHS BY ZEVA OELBAUM

HarperCollinsPublishers

HarperCollins books may be purchased for educational, business, or sales promotional use. For information please write: Special Markets Department, HarperCollins Publishers Inc., 10 East 53rd Street, New York, NY 10022.

Printed on acid-free paper

FIRST EDITION

Designed by Joel Avirom and Jason Snyder

Design assistant: Meghan Day Healey

Library of Congress Cataloging-in-Publication Data
Cost, Bruce, 1945–
    Big bowl noodles and rice : fresh Asian cooking from the renowned restaurant / Bruce Cost, with Matt McMillin.
        p. cm.
ISBN 0-06-019420-0
    1. Cookery, Asian. 2. Cookery (Pasta) 3. Cookery (Rice) I. McMillin, Matt, 1970–   II. Big Bowl (Firm) III. Title.

TX725.5.AI C69 2000
641.595—dc21

                                              00-025543

00 01 02 03 04 RRD 10 9 8 7 6 5 4 3 2 1

For Jennifer, Eliza,
Ben, and Madeline

CONTENTS

ACKNOWLEDGMENTS

More than an author's recipe collection, this book is the product of painfully honest feedback from several sources, all of whom need to be thanked. Foremost, with four busy restaurants at the time these dishes were tested, it is the public who tells you what they like by ordering it or, what they don't like by ignoring it. So thanks to Big Bowl customers who provide daily statistics detailing what has appeal.

Second, but also foremost, are the four other working partners in this venture: credited on the cover is Executive Chef Matt McMillin, a big, sweet guy with a passionate devotion to knowing all he can about this food and to teaching it to his minions. The others, Dan Ormond, Ginna Shannon, and Kevin Brown (who conceived of Big Bowl), provide constant support if not affection, and are not above paging you from the upstairs dining room to say, "You know you really ought to change these crab cakes"; or, by the same token, "This chow fun is phenomenal."

Thanks to the chefs, a diverse and wonderful crew not above giving a little feedback themselves: Keith Wood, who moved his family from California to Chicago; Raul Gutierrez, who tested many of these recipes; Octavio Paz; and Mike Bellovich. Special thanks to a duo who relentlessly pursue excellence for Big Bowl, Geoff Alexander and Drew Gass; as well as to Big Bowl pioneers Julie Chickola, Amanda Su, Michael Micek, Brian Portman, Vanessa Miller, Amy Nemitz, and all Big Bowl employees.

A heartfelt expression of appreciation to the people at Brinker International, especially Norman Brinker, Ron McDougall, Doug Brooks, Russell Owens, and Starlette Johnson for providing us with the means, guidance, and support to grow.

Thanks to Lettuce Entertain You's Steve Ottmann, Howard Katz, Jay Stieber, Gerard Centioli, Steve Donahue, and Tom Muno, who work behind the scenes on our behalf, and to all Lettuce employees. (A personal note of thanks to Ann Johnson.)

The warmest gratitude to editor Susan Friedland and to agent Doe Coover. Thank you to Rich Melman, who, in November 1995, first tasted this food and decided we should all take a shot at it.

ix

INTRODUCTION

Simply stated, this book is a collection of appetizers, noodle dishes, and stir-frys for the home cook, adapted from the menu and specials of the popular Big Bowl restaurants. Because of my own history with this food, however, I'd like to go beyond that and put the book and the restaurants that spawned it in historical perspective.

What follows will be a little personal, but I'll state from the outset that whatever success the Big Bowls enjoy can be found in the timely combination of the food I've loved, cooked, and promoted for around three decades with the expertise of the restaurant group Lettuce Entertain You that has been honing its skills for just about as long.

Thirty years ago Asian food occupied a small, exotic niche in America. In New York where I was living, people had just discovered there was Chinese cooking other than Cantonese-American. The first Sichuan restaurants opened and, since Americans seemed to like spice, Hunan restaurants followed. To distinguish their food from "Cantonese," Chinese restaurants offered what they called "Mandarin cooking." Dishes such as Hot and Sour Soup, Mu Shu Pork, and General Tso's Chicken replaced Sweet and Sour Pork and Egg Rolls. Dim Sum restaurants opened in big-city China-towns and, if you knew where to go, it was possible to get decent renditions of Shanghai's famous soup dumplings, *shaolin bao*, or a Taiwanese breakfast featuring *yu taio* (fried crullers) served with *doujiang* (salty soybean soup). Even the fare of the Chinese Hakka people, whose hardscrabble existence as itinerant field workers led them to subsist imaginatively on "delicacies" such as spinal column, dried fish lips, various pickles, and a lot of bean curd, could be found, modified for American tastes, in newly opened Hakka restaurants on both coasts.

We discovered new Chinese provinces through new restaurants offering that food, likewise the countries of Southeast Asia. People discussed the differences between Thai and Laotian cooking, no matter that there was a shaky connection between what was served on these shores and the native cooking. At the time, a friend who is an Asian-languages scholar led a tour of people mostly from the Upper West Side of Manhattan to Chengdu in Sichuan, China, where they had a banquet. In that part of

New York an average of one restaurant per block had opened billing itself as Sichuan, so these people were sure of themselves when they proclaimed, loudly, that what they were being served in Chengdu was not Sichuan food.

While gaining wider and wider exposure to mostly urban Americans, until recently Asian food hadn't really made a leap into the mainstream. Still served for the most part in inexpensive ethnic venues in Asian enclaves in big cities, the Asian food in these restaurants simply expanded the Asian-American repertoire.

Until recently, those of us who spent the past twenty to thirty years cooking and writing about Asian food were a tiny, not-quite-legitimate minority. We watched Italian food move on from the fare served on red-checkered tablecloths at Italian-American restaurants to the authentically regional in newly designed restaurants by owners with no Italian heritage. Mediterranean-style food with its emphasis on fresh, fine ingredients was wholeheartedly adopted and became California or New American cooking as young American chefs, olive oil in hand, made this food our own.

For whatever reason—exposure to Asian food via new immigrants, travel to Asia, saturation of Mediterranean-style cooking, a new generation—times have changed. Young American cooks are opening restaurants featuring Asian food and, if not, they're adopting Asian ingredients into their cooking. It makes sense since we're talking about the world's oldest, most varied cuisines. Although it's the last substantive niche to be explored by our cooks, adopting techniques and ingredients that have been enjoyed by billions over millennia is a pretty safe bet and is, perhaps, inevitable.

As I write this, it's Tuesday night at Big Bowl, and I've just picked my way through a throng of young Chicagoans, many of whom will wait up to an hour for the opportunity to enjoy fresh Chinese egg noodles with peanut sauce, or stir-fried with blackened chiles and chicken; hand-cut Shanghai Noodles with Vegetables and Eggplant (page 86); Pad Thai rice noodles with shrimp; beef with Chinese broccoli in Shaoxing rice wine sauce; and a real Kung Pao chicken with fermented chili paste and whole bean sauce. Not far away in Minneapolis—in this nation's heartland—people are packing into a Big Bowl there.

I mention this not so much to boast, but as an expression of amazement at what appears to be a profound shift in the taste of Americans, particularly the young and educated. After a 2,100-year reign as Asia's most beloved man-made staple, noodles would seem to be on their way to becoming American, like pizza. At Big Bowl we

know this not only from trade magazine articles about the proliferation of noodle shops and other Asian restaurants in New York, California, and increasingly across the land but because, as of this writing, the customers at four restaurants are slurping down one ton of Chinese egg noodles, Shanghai wheat noodles, and two kinds of slippery rice noodles every three days. They also take them out, and we deliver them to their door.

For those unfamiliar with Big Bowl, the menu offers about seventy-five items—mostly noodles (five kinds), stir-fries, and "little dishes to share"— with additional specials that change weekly. If the customers need heat, they find on the table a fiery condiment that we make every couple of days from fresh and dried chile peppers. We squeeze lemons every day for use in our Thai dishes, and our Thai curry pastes are made from scratch starting with the toasting and grinding of whole spices. We even make the ginger ale from fresh ginger.

Why this book? It was suggested that much of the appeal of Big Bowl's food is the feeling, "I can make this." It's authentic and accessible at the same time. It's fresh and healthy, full-flavored Chinese and Southeast Asian food, much of it meal-in-a bowl. It's food that translates easily to the home kitchen. We're hoping the book is useful for those who can't always get to Big Bowl. We want to share because all we really try do is serve great home-style cooking in a restaurant.

SPECIAL INGREDIENTS

(What You'll Need to Know to Cook from This Book)

FRESH INGREDIENTS

Herbs and Fresh Seasonings

THAI OR "ASIAN" BASIL—a tropical variety of sweet basil with small green leaves, purple stems and flowers, and a wonderful basil/anise flavor; the Thais call this *bai horapa* and the Vietnamese, *rau hung*. Available in Southeast Asian markets year round, it can be stored for a couple of days in the refrigerator with the stems in water and leaves loosely covered with a plastic bag.

MINT—You may use any fresh spearmint for the recipes in this book. Southeast Asian markets carry a fuzzy-leafed tropical variety sold in bunches with stems up to a foot long. Unlike its cousin, basil, mint is not usually cooked; rather it's used in salads.

CHILE PEPPERS—At Big Bowl we prefer a red hot pepper from California called a "fresno." About 2 to 2½ inches long and conical in shape, this provides fire without being blistering, and it has a sweet, fresh-pepper taste. We also recommend long, thin cayenne and serrano peppers, although the latter's small size makes it time-consuming to prepare. Jalapeño's familiar Mexican-style flavor, while good, tastes somewhat alien in Thai and Chinese dishes.

CORIANDER (CILANTRO)—This, the world's most popular herb, is available any-where; store it with its stems in water and leaves loosely covered with a plastic bag.

GINGER—Ginger is available in most supermarkets and groceries. Buy it fresh (it should feel hard) and leave it out on the counter where it will keep for a week or so. If you want to refrigerate it, wrap it in a paper towel in a plastic bag that is loosely sealed. Peel before using.

GALANGAL—Called "Thai ginger" or *kha* by the Thais, this ginger relative has a more medicinal, camphorous taste than ginger. Available fresh at Southeast Asian markets, it spoils quicker than ginger and should be wrapped in a paper towel and kept in a unsealed plastic bag in the refrigerator. Unlike ginger, it's not usually eaten except when ground in curries, as a slice of it has the texture of a wood chip. It traditionally flavors soups and stews.

LEMONGRASS—Another strictly Southeast Asian herb, this 2-foot gray-green stalk is available year round in Thai, Cambodian, and Vietnamese markets. Having a balm-like lemon fragrance, familiar to us from soaps and other cosmetics that are laced with it, only 6 inches of its bulbous base should be used, either minced for salads and stir-frys, or sliced for soups. It must be used immediately after cutting before its flavor vanishes. Dried lemongrass is ineffective.

CHINESE CHIVES—Sold in bunches of about 3 inches in diameter in Asian markets, this plant has grassy, flat, dark green leaves, and a delicately sweet flavor when cooked; we add it from time to time to curried noodles. Refrigerate and use quickly after buying as these chives don't keep well; after a few days they'll make their presence known.

TAMARIND—Although tamarind pods are available in Southeast Asian and Mexican markets—they're 3 to 4 inches long, flat, and grayish brown—we buy the pulp, from Thailand, which has been removed from these pods and packaged in 8-ounce plastic-wrapped blocks. It is dark brown and has a prune-like sour-sweet taste. Look for those with a little give—they should not be brick-hard. Tamarind at Big Bowl is used mostly to marinate satays (see page 21). To prepare, put the pulp in a saucepan, cover with water, and heat. Cook, stirring until soft, about 10 minutes. Then pour it through a strainer, working it with your fingers into the mesh to remove all that is flavorful. Seeds and strings should be left behind.

BAMBOO SHOOTS—Although they show up fresh and unhusked from time to time in Asian markets, whole canned shoots are not a terrible substitute as the fresh often have to be boiled anyway to rid them of their acrid flavor. After you open the can, leftover shoots can be kept up to a week, refrigerated in cold water that should be changed every couple of days. Slice as directed in the recipes. Companion and Ma Ling are two fine brands among others.

Cabbages

BOK CHOY (SHANGHAI)—We recommend this widely available variety of bok choy that has uniform, light green stems and spoon-shaped leaves, and is harvested as a baby plant of about 6 inches. Brilliant green when cooked, this is delicious in stir-fries with a delicate flavor and a soft but crisp texture. To prepare, trim away any unwanted outer leaves, trim the base, and slice the plant into quarters lengthwise. The more common variety of bok choy with its white stems and dark green leaves can be substituted. If you can find it, the baby variety, under 6 inches in height is preferable. Keep this in the crisper as you would any vegetable.

CHINESE BROCCOLI—This dull green plant, called *gai lan* by the Cantonese, has fewer flower clusters and more leaves (meant to be eaten) than Western broccoli. It is one of the world's most calcium-laden vegetables, high in iron and vitamins A and C. We use it rather than Western broccoli for our menu items. Slightly earthier and a smidgen more bitter than broccoli, it has an affinity for oyster sauce and can be blanched before it's stir-fried. It's the only vegetable we offer cooked by itself.

NAPA CABBAGE—Sometimes called celery cabbage, this is a staple of northern China just as the bok choys (also cabbage-family members) are in the south. It is the most delicately flavored cabbage and may be steamed, stir-fried, braised, or used in soups. Store it loosely wrapped in plastic in the refrigerator.

CHINESE MUSTARD GREENS—We use these, called *gai choy,* in some winter stir-fries, sometimes sliced and cured briefly by salting. Mustard greens have a spicy bite and should be prepared and stored like any cabbage.

ASIAN RADISH OR DAIKON (JAPANESE)—Widely used by the Chinese, Japanese, and Koreans. We use this hefty white root in our winter braised or stir-fried dishes, and we also make a Shanghainese fresh pickle out of it (Spicy Daikon and Carrot Pickle, page 55). When cooked it has a soft, refreshing taste and absorbs the flavors of any rich meat it's cooked with. It is thought to aid in digesting anything oily. The radish should be peeled before using.

Other Vegetables

ASIAN EGGPLANT—We use the long, thin, lavender variety called Chinese eggplant in our cooking simply because it's sweet, tender, and relatively seedless compared to Western eggplant, and it needn't be salted to extract bitter juices. Just cut it up and use it. Not at all Mediterranean, this eggplant is native to Southeast Asia, where it still grows wild.

BEAN SPROUTS—Nutritious and rich in vitamin C, this is an instant vegetable that doesn't require proper weather or a patch of land. It can be bought fresh daily at Asian markets. The common variety is sprouted from the green mung bean. Look for those that are crisp and white, without a trace of brown at the stem or root. When cooking with noodles, these are best tossed in just as the heat is turned off before plating.

SNOW PEAS, SNAP PEAS—Best fresh-picked, these need to be crisp and sweet when raw. They also need to be strung by pinching off a bit of the tip and pulling down one side; then repeating at the other end and side.

WATER CHESTNUTS—Although they may be the least popular ingredient with any kitchen crew because of the time it takes to peel them, fresh water chestnuts are a must for the recipes that require them because of their coconut-like taste and crunch. Using these fresh in dishes is a plus for Big Bowl customers as most Asian-American restaurants serve the canned variety, which are insipid. They are found year round in Chinese markets; look for those that are rock hard with a slight sheen to the skin.

To peel, first rinse them of any mud, cut off the flat top and bottom, then pare the circular edge with a small knife. Keep them briefly in cold water until ready to use. (Avoid those showing up increasingly in Cryovac as they have been treated with a chemical to retard spoilage that ruins their taste.)

PRESERVED AND PROCESSED INGREDIENTS

DRIED BLACK MUSHROOMS—Known as shiitake (Japan) or *dong-gu* (China), these are the oldest cultivated mushrooms, no longer found in the wild. While they can be bought fresh these days, the top grades in Asia are always grown to be dried. Superior varieties, with thick, white-cracked caps, sell for over $30 a pound. Considered as much a flavoring as an ingredient, they're available in varying grades in most Asian markets, with the best sold in Chinese herbal shops. They keep well in a covered jar or plastic container without refrigeration.

To soak, cover with hot water and let stand for at least 30 minutes. After soaking, squeeze the mushrooms over the soaking bowl—reserve the liquid for vegetarian stock (see page 66) or to be used in place of chicken stock—and then cut off the woody stems. Slice according to directions.

DRIED SHRIMP—More of a flavoring than a shrimp substitute, these are important to Thai and Vietnamese dishes especially and are a staple in China as well. We use them mostly ground (we grind them in a spice grinder) in the Thai cucumber salad we serve with chicken satays, our Vietnamese Fried Rice (page 157) and our Chinese Sticky Rice Packages (page 118). Buy bigger, softer varieties that cost over $12 per pound in Asian markets. The small, cheap ones have an unpleasant, funky taste. Dried shrimp can be stored unrefrigerated, away from light, in a covered jar.

SICHUAN PRESERVED VEGETABLE—A thick, lump-like stem from a kind of mustard native to Sichuan, these are cured in salt and chili powder. When chopped and simmered in water, they yield a tasty stock, which is the way we use these at Big Bowl (see All-Vegetable Wonton Soup, page 66). Available in Chinese markets, these are sometimes sold in bulk in large crocks but reliably can be bought in 12-ounce red-and-yellow cans labeled SZECHUAN PRESERVED VEGETABLE. Store in the refrigerator in a covered jar.

CHINESE SWEET SAUSAGE—Reddish, marbled with fat, and known as *lop chong* in Cantonese, these are available in 1-pound packages in Chinese markets. Some big-city Chinatowns—New York, San Francisco, Vancouver—have their own sausage makers. They're sweet and especially popular with non-Asians as well. Before slicing for fried rice for example—they're great in scrambled eggs—steam for 5 minutes with a little water in a small covered pot.

Asian Dairy

COCONUT MILK—Not the liquid inside the coconut, rather, this is the freshly grated meat infused with hot water and then wrung out. As with cow's milk, the cream rises to the top as coconut milk sits, and it is chemically closer to butterfat than to vegetable fat. Like dairy to Northern Europeans, it is a vital staple of Southeast Asia but not particularly cared for or used much by most Chinese. We recommend a wonderful canned variety available at Southeast Asian and some Chinese markets, Chaokoh, from Thailand. When the can is opened, the fat and liquid should be mixed as they may have separated. Use as directed in this book.

BEAN CURD (TOFU)—The nutritious and easily digestible soybean product called bean curd or *doufu* by the Chinese is most desirable when freshly made and is sold in bulk in Chinese communities. (New York's Chinatown may have the best.) Barring that, acceptable products are sold fresh in 1-pound plastic packages at many supermarkets. We use a hard variety. Once open, bean curd should be transferred to a bowl and covered with fresh cold water.

Soy Sauces

SALTED AND FERMENTED BLACK BEANS OR CHINESE BLACK BEANS—The first soy bean seasoning, whose use antedates liquid soy sauce, these little salted and cured black soybeans have a pleasing winy flavor that is especially great with seafood. Meats, chicken, and vegetables, particularly asparagus and broccoli, also have an affinity for their special flavor. Once used throughout China, black beans are now a staple in Southern Chinese (Cantonese) seasoning.

They're widely available in plastic packages at Chinese markets. We use Yang Jiang brand, which comes from China in a 17-ounce cylindrical box. To use, after mashing lightly with the back of a large spoon, they can be simply added to a dish whole, without rinsing. They keep indefinitely, stored away from light and heat in a covered jar.

BEAN SAUCE—Another ancient sauce whose use preceded liquid soy sauce, this lumpy paste, sometimes called "brown bean sauce," is made from whole soybeans, salted and fermented, a flavor familiar to those who know Western and Northern Chinese food. It's a staple of our Sichuan dishes such as Sichuan Garlic Noodles with Blackened Chiles and Peanuts (page 80). We use Koon Chun Sauce Factory's Bean Sauce, not to be confused with their Ground Bean Sauce, which is much saltier.

HOISIN SAUCE—Sweet, garlicky, and spiced, this flavored and sweetened version of ground bean sauce is popular in the West and, as such, is kind of an Asian ketchup. We serve it with our Loin of Lamb Mu Shu Wrap (page 46).

SOY SAUCE—This staple is indispensable for Chinese cooking, and we use only Chinese soy sauces, of which two varieties are required by the recipes in this book:

Chinese Light Soy Sauce—Not to be confused with low-sodium varieties and used mostly in Southern China, this soy sauce is preferred by the Chinese for dip sauces and with seafood and vegetable dishes. We use Koon Chun Sauce Factory's Thin Soy. Pearl River Bridge's Superior Soy is also fine.

Chinese Dark Soy Sauce—This soy sauce is aged longer than light soy sauce. Toward the end of its brewing (soy sauce is brewed and aged), bead molasses is added, which gives it a darker caramel-like color. Used primarily in Northern China, this is called for mostly in dishes with red meats such as beef, pork, and lamb. We use Pearl River Bridge's Mushroom Soy.

Fish Sauces

FISH SAUCE—Called *nuoc mam* by the Vietnamese and *nam pla* by the Thais, this is the soy sauce of Southeast Asia and, in fact, stems from the same technology—that is, it is a fermented and aged protein product with high nutritional value. Here anchovies are used instead of soybeans. As with soy sauce, it's one of the two or three most important staples in Asian cooking.

Although the smell of fish sauce is off-putting, the flavor it lends to dishes has been well received by the mainstream if the popularity of Big Bowl is any indication. In fact, our dip sauces contain a higher proportion of it (more akin to how it's actually used in Asia) than is found in most Thai-American and Vietnamese-American restaurants.

We recommend and use two Vietnamese-style fish sauces: Viet Huong Three Crabs Brand, and Flying Lion Phu Quoc.

GROUND FISH SAUCE—(*Mam Nem*) Our curries call for a "creamed anchovy" kind of sauce that is available in 7-ounce bottles in Southeast Asian markets. (We also have used it in a mock Caesar salad, page 59). Numerous brands are available.

OYSTER SAUCE—This staple of Cantonese restaurants has been familiar to Americans since the first chop suey houses. It's an excellent all-purpose seasoning for noodles, meat, seafood, and vegetable dishes. Made of oysters, water, and salt with some natural caramel, you get what you pay for in terms of real oyster flavor. Available in 14-ounce bottles, buy the most expensive, the best being Sa Cheng's Oyster Flavored Sauce from China. If you can't find that, buy the most expensive Hong Kong brand you can find. We get a natural product made and packaged for us in Shenzhen, China. This sauce, Triwell, is, as yet, unavailable in retail stores. Oyster sauce is for sale in all Chinese and Southeast Asian markets and is usually carried in Japanese and Korean food stores as well.

OTHER SAUCES, VINEGAR, SPIRITS

CHILI PASTE WITH GARLIC—Fermented like soy sauce, and with a wonderful winy and garlicky chile flavor that is the essence of Sichuan cooking, we recommend Lan Chi's Chili Paste with Garlic from Taiwan, available in 8-ounce jars. Barring that, buy Szechuan Chili Sauce, in black 6-ounce cans. (At Big Bowl we use these in our Sichuan cooking but make from scratch the chile condiment we put on the tables.)

VINEGAR—We use both Japanese Rice Vinegar (Marukan) and good Western-style red wine vinegar in the cooking at Big Bowl, and we call for both in the recipes in this book.

SHAOXING RICE WINE—Amber-colored and akin to a dry sherry, this is the world's oldest continuously brewed wine, made on China's East Coast in Shaoxing. It is drunk both warm, like Japanese sake, or cold, and is cooked with extensively in Eastern China. We call for a splash or two to finish many of the dishes in this book. A drinkable dry sherry may be substituted. In some states such as California, you can buy this in a Chinese grocery store. In states such as New York and Illinois, you must go to a liquor store that carries Chinese alcoholic beverages. Avoid the salted "cooking wine" varieties. The brand we use is Pagoda Shao Xing Rice Wine from China.

SPICES AND OTHER INGREDIENTS

Spices

STAR ANISE—Called for in some of our seasoning mixtures for poultry (see Five Spice Whole Chicken with Sticky Rice Packages, page 117, or Roast Duck with Ginger-Orange Glaze, page 120), this licorice-flavored pod of a Chinese evergreen is one of the few real spices the Chinese use. It's available in Chinese and Vietnamese markets in 4-ounce bags.

CASSIA (CHINESE CINNAMON)—What's sold in the United States as cinnamon is usually this coarser relative that the Chinese use to spice meat and poultry dishes. Like cinnamon, it's a bark that comes in curled pieces or "quills," and is sold in small packages in Chinese and Vietnamese markets.

SICHUAN PEPPERCORNS—This native of Sichuan China is a small dried berry unrelated to the common peppercorn and is numbing like mild novocaine, rather than spicy hot.

An ancient Chinese seasoning and former table condiment, it is toasted before use and is a popular seasoning with fried and roasted foods. It is also infused in chili oils. Before grinding, it should be heated and shaken in a small pan until it smokes. It's sold in Chinese markets, usually in 8-ounce plastic packages.

Other Ingredients

SESAME OIL—Primarily used as a flavoring, this seductively flavored oil, made from toasted and crushed sesame seeds, is a wonderful addition to Chinese rice and noodle dishes, soups, and dip sauces. We recommend and use Kadoya from Japan.

CHILI OIL—Although sold commercially, sometimes under the name "Sa-te oil," I've found what's on the store shelves too often rancid. We call for this from time to time in our dip sauces, and at Big Bowl we make our own.

To make chili oil, chop 1 cup of dried red chile peppers to a coarse grind in a spice grinder. Place them in a stainless steel saucepan with ¾ cup of fine peanut oil (see Cooking Oil, below) and heat slowly until the peppers begin to foam. Keep cooking and the moment small dark flecks of pepper on the side of the pan begin to blacken, turn off the heat, cover, and let sit, 2 to 4 hours. Strain the oil into a jar and store away from the light.

YELLOW ROCK SUGAR—A crystallized blend of refined and unrefined sugar and honey, rock sugar is necessary for the succulent braised dishes of Eastern China, usually duck, pork, or other rich meats. We call for it in the Braised Short Ribs with Noodles recipe (page 147).

It sells in Chinese and Southeast Asian markets for under $1.00 for a 1-pound box or bag. To use, simply add a lump that approximates what the recipe calls for.

PEANUTS—At Big Bowl we make peanut sauces from scratch (page 62), starting with a peeled and husked peanut that is briefly blanched. They're available by the pound in Asian markets.

COOKING OIL—We recommend peanut oil for frying and stir-frying. We use a wonderfully fragrant, cold-pressed variety for many of our dishes from Lion & Globe of Hong Kong. Recognizing that some people are seriously allergic to peanuts, we keep other oils on hand.

RICE—We use long-grain Jasmine rice from Thailand. For the glutinous "sticky rice" we use a Chinese-style short-grain variety packaged by Koda Farms in California. The Vietnamese Fried Rice in this book (page 157) calls for a black glutinous rice (with the bran layer still attached) from Thailand that is sold in Southeast Asian markets.

2 NOODLES
(Varieties, How to Cook, Substitutes)

We call for four kinds of noodles in this book: two fresh wheat flour noodles, one fresh rice flour noodle, and one dried rice flour noodle. All can be found in Asian markets. These are each described below along with how they should be cooked and acceptable substitutions.

CHINESE WHEAT FLOUR NOODLES (FRESH)—Sold in Asian markets in 1-pound bags, these noodles come in a variety of shapes and thicknesses and are either *egg and wheat flour (egg noodles)* or just *wheat flour*. At Big Bowl we use two kinds: Chinese egg noodles and Shanghai-style noodles:

Chinese Egg Noodles—By far the most popular noodle at Big Bowl, these are most familiar to non-Asians as they resemble spaghetti. Popularly sold as *mein* (pronounced "mean") in Chinese markets, these are also known as *ramen* to the Japanese and *ba mee* to the Thais. We use "regular *mein*," about ⅛ inch thick, which are sold in 1-pound packages in the noodle section of Asian groceries. The best are pale yellow in color (bright yellow indicates coloring—check the package), have a dry, fresh appearance, and should not look mashed and damp. These are conducive to stir-frying or pan-frying, or can be served cold with a peanut–sesame sauce topping. All three techniques are called for in this book.

NOTE: Chinese egg noodles are also sold "thin" or "extra-thin" for soups or pan-frying. They also come in a flat fettuccine-like shape, which are best stir-fried, or cooked and topped with a sauce.

TO COOK FRESH CHINESE EGG NOODLES: Bring a large quantity of water to a boil—add the noodles but not salt or oil—and cook to taste, at least 4 to 6 minutes. Chinese do not like noodles al dente; they should be cooked just beyond that point. Before stir-frying, pan-frying, or putting in soup, in other words, the way they are called for in the recipes that follow, the noodles should be cooked as above, run under cold water to stop the cooking, and tossed with a little oil to prevent them from clumping, about 2 teaspoons (peanut or sesame) per pound of cooked noodles.

TO SUBSTITUTE FOR CHINESE EGG NOODLES YOU MAY USE THE FOLLOWING:

Plain Fresh Chinese Wheat Flour Noodles—Minus the egg, these noodles also come in a spaghetti shape as do the egg noodles, except they're an off-white color. Prepare the same way.

Dried Chinese Wheat Flour or Egg Noodles—The same noodles sold fresh in Chinese markets can be purchased dried in 1-pound packages, either in straight 12-inch lengths or, in the case of some egg noodles, in swirls.

TO COOK CHINESE DRIED NOODLES: Proceed as you would for the fresh noodles, but boil for a longer period of time; ignore the cooking instructions on the package, trusting instead your own taste.

Italian Spaghetti—If you can't get those above, use these.

Shanghai-Style Noodles—One of the most popular regional varieties of Chinese wheat noodles is this thick and beautiful, oval-shaped noodle that has a crooked hand-cut look. A relative of the Japanese *udon* noodle, we use these in meal-in-a-bowl soups as well as in various stir-fried dishes. This book calls for them to be used both ways. While not as widely available as the egg noodles above, they're for sale in most Asian markets that display a noodle section.

TO COOK FRESH SHANGHAI NOODLES: Bring a large quantity of water to a boil—don't add salt or oil—and cook to taste, at least 6 to 8 minutes. They should be beyond al dente. After cooking as above, and before stir-frying or adding to soup, the way they are called for in the recipes here, run under cold water to stop the cooking, and toss with a little oil to prevent them from clumping, about 2 teaspoons of oil (peanut or sesame) per pound of cooked noodles.

TO SUBSTITUTE FOR FRESH SHANGHAI NOODLES YOU MAY USE THE FOLLOWING:

Dried Chinese Noodles—Round dried noodles approximating the thickness of Shanghai noodles can be purchased dried in 1-pound packages, usually in straight 12-inch lengths. A thick slightly flat variety is also acceptable.

TO COOK DRIED CHINESE NOODLES: Proceed as you would for the fresh noodles, but boil for a longer period; ignore the cooking instructions on the package trusting instead your own taste.

Dried Japanese Udon—These are thick white noodles made of wheat flour, salt, and water; they come both flat and round. Dried, they're sold in packages of 12 ounces or 1 pound. Cook as you would any dried noodle.

Dried Fettuccine—In a pinch these will work in the stir-fry dishes.

RICE FLOUR NOODLES—We use two rice noodles at Big Bowl, both made from rice flour, and both are called for in this book:

Pad Thai Noodles—Known also as "rice sticks," as well as *banh pho* (Vietnamese) and *jantabon* (Thai), these are sold in 1-pound packages in Chinese, Thai, and Vietnamese markets. You'll want the thin flat noodles as opposed to the thin round ones. We use Erawan Brand with *vermicelle de riz* on the label. These are soaked in hot water rather than cooked before using.

TO SOAK PAD THAI RICE NOODLES: Put the noodles in a bowl and cover with hot tap water (about 110 degrees), and then allow to sit for 30 minutes. Rinse with cold water after soaking.

Fresh Wide Rice Noodles—Called or labeled *Ho Fun*, or *Ho Fan*, these thick noodles, sold fresh in rectangular whole sheets in Chinese markets, are affectionately called "big rice noodles" at Big Bowl. Used in Chow Fun dishes or dishes that call for "big rice noodles" in this book (page 102), these may be cut to any width. For most dishes we cut them 1 inch wide; for length, we cut them at the folds (they're folded in the packages they come in), which results in a noodle about 6 inches long. Made locally in Chicago under the brand name Quon Yick, these are freshly made by noodle-makers in Chinese communities around the country. They will keep refrigerated for about a week.

NOTE: These need not be cooked or oiled before using in stir-fried dishes; they are usually sold pre-oiled in markets. Before using and after cutting, be sure the noodles are well separated before cooking; to be added to soups, they should be boiled first for 20 seconds or so.

TO SUBSTITUTE FOR FRESH WIDE RICE NOODLES YOU MAY USE THE FOLLOWING:

Fresh Wheat Flour Chow Fun Noodles—Some Chinese markets carry a fresh Chow Fun noodle made from wheat flour and sold in 1-pound packages. About ¾ of an inch wide, these can be substituted for the "big rice noodles" on page 12. They should be boiled and prepared like the Shanghai noodles.

Dried Wide Rice Flour Noodles—Not a terrific substitute, these should be soaked like the Pad Thai noodles in hot tap water for 30 minutes or more, then drained and lightly oiled.

HOW TO COOK WITH THIS BOOK

EQUIPMENT

You will not need anything special to cook from this book. A large skillet or wok of at least 14 inches will do. (At Big Bowl restaurants, most of our dishes are stir-fried (sautéed) in a 12-inch wok-like pan on top of a stove.)

RECOMMENDED: While it looks cumbersome, a 16-inch wok is the most versatile for Asian cooking. You can always cook a small amount in a large wok but not the reverse; and a larger wok can be used for steaming—you need a rack (a perforated disk or round pie rack) to suspend the food over the boiling water; and you need a cover. A 16-inch spun steel wok (it needs to be seasoned) with cover and steaming rack is inexpensive.

FOR STEAMING: The 16-inch wok with a rack and cover as described above is recommended. There are also bamboo steamer layers with covers available that can be inserted into a large wok, and large aluminum steamers with two layers and a cover are for sale wherever Asian cooking equipment is sold.

FOR FRYING: Only a few dishes in this book are deep-fried, that is, cooked until golden in a large amount of oil. For these we recommend a wok and a skimmer or large round perforated spoon available at Asian hardware stores or cooking equipment dealers. (Ironically more oil ensures that fried food will be golden brown and dry, not greasy, because the oil temperature can be maintained. Adding cold food to a small amount of oil lowers the temperature, allowing the oil to penetrate the food.)

SPECIAL TECHNIQUES

Roughly speaking, 80 percent of the noodle and rice dish recipes require the following steps:

1   Marinating the meat or seafood and briefly cooking it in oil (called "passing"—this is discussed further on page 15)

2   Heating the cooking pan and adding the cooking oil

3   Adding fresh ingredients: first, such seasonings as ginger and garlic; second, vegetables

4 Adding any stock or sauce mixture

5 Adding precooked noodles (if used); and meat or seafood cooked in Step #1

6 Stirring (or tossing if you're adept with a pan) until hot

7 Plating and garnishing

Step #1 (Passing) At the beginning of many of the recipes, the meat, poultry, or seafood is marinated in a little cornstarch and sesame oil, then passed briefly through a quantity of warm to hot oil and drained. At Big Bowl we follow this refined, traditional Chinese technique because it results in plump, juicier shrimp, chicken, and beef. The marinade both seals in the juices and tenderizes. It's an option we recommend but *you can choose to simply add the meat to the oil after the fresh seasonings* in Step #3 above; stir until the meat or seafood just changes color, and continue until the end. You'll get a fine dish.

Step #6 During this step some saucier dishes require thickening with a little cornstarch mixed with water. This is done to give those dishes a glossy sheen, indicating that the sauce is coating the ingredients. (These sauces should not be thick or gloppy.)

STOCK FOR SOUPS AND COOKING

A good chicken stock is fundamental to many of the recipes in this book. Every day at each Big Bowl we make a gigantic kettle of stock with over 200 pounds of meaty chicken backs and bones. To ensure that it is crystal clear, we skim it carefully and simmer it slowly, and to make certain it is full-flavored and complex, we use a high ratio of meaty fresh bones to water.

To Make Your Own Chicken Stock:

Put equal amounts of fresh chicken bones, including backs, necks, wing tips, etc., and water in a pot with a slice of ginger and bring to a boil. When it boils, skim the foam from the surface until it disappears, then reduce the heat to simmer, cover, and cook for 3 to 4 hours. Turn off the heat and let sit until nearly cool, then strain and refrigerate. Stock will keep in the refrigerator if brought to a boil every 3 days, or you may freeze it. Some markets carry fresh chicken stock; recommended canned brands are College Inn and Swanson's.

Some of our recipes require Thai herb and spice mixtures we call "curries," and while you can use curry powder (in half the amount called for in the recipes) and Thai markets sell canned curry pastes, we highly recommend using the following recipes for the dishes in this book that call for them. These clean-tasting curry pastes, we feel, distinguish the food at Big Bowl:

Thai cooking is an amalgam of both Indian and Chinese influences. Part of the legacy of India is the various curry pastes the Thais use. These usually combine traditional Indian spices such as coriander and cumin seed with Thai seasonings such as lemongrass, galangal, and fish paste. Here are two authentic varieties we use at Big Bowl, which are called for by recipes in this book. Rather than a powder, or something from a can, these are made from scratch and they give a lively, clean taste to the dishes they're used in. Not difficult, they're well worth the effort. It should be noted that the "red" in Red Curry Paste refers to the dried red chiles; Yellow Curry Paste also has dried red chiles, but has a different spice configuration including the yellow provided by the turmeric.

Yellow Curry Paste

○

30 dried red chiles

¼ cup coriander seeds

4 teaspoons cumin seeds

2 teaspoons black peppercorns

1 tablespoon powdered turmeric

3 tablespoons chopped fresh galangal

2 bunches coriander (roots and 1 inch of stems only)

15 garlic cloves

⅔ cup chopped shallots

3 stalks lemongrass (bottom 2 inches only)

¾ cup peanut oil

1 tablespoon kosher salt

3 tablespoons *mam nem* ground fish sauce

2 tablespoons fresh lemon juice

Over medium heat in a small skillet, toast the dried chiles, coriander seeds, cumin seeds, and peppercorns until fragrant. Grind to a medium powder in a spice grinder or blender. Add the turmeric to the spice mixture.

Put the galangal, coriander, garlic, shallots, lemongrass, and ¼ cup of the peanut oil in a food processor and grind to a paste. Add the spice powder, salt, fish sauce, and lemon juice and continue to blend. Remove the paste to a bowl and stir in the remaining ½ cup oil. Transfer to a jar and refrigerate. It will keep a week or so.

Makes about 2 cups

Red Curry Paste

20 dried red chile peppers

¼ cup coriander seeds

2 tablespoons cumin seeds

1 tablespoon black peppercorns

3 stalks lemongrass (bottom
    2 inches on stalk only)

5 slices fresh galangal

4 fresh red chile peppers

8 garlic cloves

½ pound shallots, peeled

1 tablespoon kosher salt

3 tablespoons *mam nem* ground fish sauce

3 tablespoons fresh lemon juice

1 teaspoon sugar

2 bunches fresh coriander
    (roots and stems only)

Grated zest of 1 lime

1 cup fine peanut oil

2 teaspoons paprika

Over medium heat in a small skillet, toast the dried chiles, coriander seeds, cumin seeds, and peppercorns until fragrant. Grind to a medium powder in a spice grinder or blender.

Put the lemongrass, galangal, fresh chiles, garlic, shallots, salt, fish sauce, lemon juice, sugar, coriander, and lime zest in a food processor and grind to a paste. Add ¼ cup of the peanut oil, the paprika, and the spice powder, and continue to blend. Remove the paste to a bowl and stir in the remaining ¾ cup oil. Transfer to a jar and refrigerate. It will keep a week or so.

Makes about 2 cups

4 HOW TO MAKE A MEAL FROM THIS BOOK

First, using this book to make even a casual home meal should be easy. There are no arcane Chinese serving rules that one has to learn because the food itself is casual—meal-in-a-bowl noodle dishes, dishes simply served with rice, and if you want tackle a meal that is slightly more elaborate for guests, there are many small appetizer-type dishes and salads. Customers at Big Bowl often make a meal of two or three small dishes, and you're free to also.

At the end of the noodle recipes and the dishes to be served with rice, you'll find for example, "Serves 2 as a complete meal or 3 to 4 as part of a larger meal." This means that if you've chosen that particular dish for a casual lunch or supper, it will satisfy two people and you won't need anything else. If it's a noodle dish, that's all you have to make; if it's a dish that goes with rice, you'll also have to cook rice (page 109).

Serving "3 to 4 as part of a larger meal," means simply that you'll need more food in the form of another dish or a couple of appetizers in addition to the recipe you've chosen to satisfy three or four diners. This extra dish need not even be Asian. It could be a salad that you like. When I did the cooking for a family of four, I would serve a dish such as Summer Chicken with Fresh-Shucked Corn and Peas (page 111), plenty of rice, and a salad.

Some recipes state only how many can be served as part of a larger meal. This is because the dish itself may require the balance of another dish to be a great meal. If it's mostly shrimp for example, such as the Shanghai Shrimp with Shiitake and Rice Wine (page 130), it's recommended that you add balance with another dish, a vegetable or chicken and vegetable dish for example.

A slightly more ambitious meal might include one of the salads in this book and one noodle dish or dish with rice. It should be stressed though that these recipes are designed to fit in with your needs and almost all can be used simply to enliven your home meals.

Although it's not the focus of the book, these recipes can certainly enliven a dinner party. You may want to start by incorporating one or two of the appetizers into a meal of your choosing, Asian or not. If you feel ready to tackle an elaborate meal, say for eight, try a first course consisting of one cold appetizer, e.g., Spring Asparagus Salad with Sesame Seeds (page 56) and one warm appetizer, such as Thai Chicken Soong (Lettuce Packages) (page 24). Follow this with two main dishes from the rice section that you feel are complementary, e.g., Sea Scallops with Tomatoes and Fresh Water Chestnuts (page 137) and Mongolian Lamb with Scallions (page 148). If you're ambitious, you can offer a noodle course before the main dishes. The good thing is, once prepared, these dishes can be cooked quickly right before serving.

It's recommended that you master these dishes one at a time before making several of them at once.

5 SMALL DISHES AND SALADS

SMALL DISHES

Skewering and grilling bite-sized pieces of meat, seafood, or vegetables is an ancient tradition spanning many cultures. The four satays that follow vary from the fanciful, like the exquisite Spring Vegetable Mushroom Satay, below, to the traditional, such as the Indonesian-style marinated chicken and beef satays.

Spring Vegetable Mushroom Satay

○

These elegant spring vegetable satays are briefly blanched to bring out their color, then brushed with a little oyster sauce and seasonings.

Twelve 12-inch bamboo skewers

6 medium to large white mushrooms, quartered

Twenty-four 2-inch scallion whites

Fresh red fresno chile peppers or bell peppers, cut into diamond-shaped 1½-inch pieces

6 large fresh shiitake mushrooms, quartered

6 small Shanghai bok choys, stripped of leaves down to a 2-inch heart and cut in half (see Note)

Twenty-four 2-inch fresh asparagus tips (see Note)

2 tablespoons oyster sauce

¼ cup light soy sauce

2 tablespoons sugar

¼ cup sesame oil

Load each skewer as follows: 1 piece each mushroom, scallion white, red pepper, shiitake, bok choy heart, 2 asparagus tips, bok choy heart, shiitake, red pepper, scallion white, white mushroom.

Mix together the oyster sauce, soy sauce, and sugar. Stir in the sesame oil. Brush the satays with this sauce, reserving the rest for a dipping sauce, and grill over medium heat, turning them once, until done. Serve with the dipping sauce on the side.

NOTE: It's helpful to blanch the bok choy and asparagus in boiling water for 30 seconds, shock them in cold water to stop the cooking, and drain and dry. This not only cooks them slightly, but maintains their bright color and moisture.

Makes 12 vegetable satays—2 per person as part of a buffet or warm-weather meal

Indonesian Chicken (or Beef) Satays with Peanut Sauce

These popular satays require an elaborate and old-fashioned preparation method employed in Malaysia and Indonesia that entails the toasting and grinding of spices and the heating and straining of tamarind pulp. For the peanut sauce dip you even start with raw peanuts. We feel it's worth it, the results being tender, flavorful grilled meats with the tastiest possible dipping sauce.

2 pounds boneless chicken breast or flank steak

Thirty-two 12-inch bamboo skewers

MARINADE

4 teaspoons coriander seeds

4 teaspoons cumin seeds

4 garlic cloves, finely minced

¼ cup brown sugar

¼ cup fish sauce

¾ cup tamarind paste (see Note)

¼ cup peanut oil

DIPPING SAUCE

½ cup fine peanut oil

½ cup raw peanuts

2 fresh serrano or fresno chiles

1 tablespoon chopped fresh ginger

4 garlic cloves

⅓ cup rich unsweetened coconut milk

1 teaspoon dark soy sauce

1 tablespoon fish sauce

1 teaspoon sugar

1 tablespoon fresh lime juice

1 teaspoon kosher salt

½ cup chopped fresh cilantro leaves

Cut approximately 1-ounce slices of meat in flat pieces (approximately 3 x ¾ inches) and thread each one onto a skewer (you'll have about 32 satays).

In a small skillet, toast the spices until fragrant, then grind to a coarse powder in a spice grinder. Mix the spices with the garlic, brown sugar, fish sauce, tamarind paste, and peanut oil. Arrange the skewers in a shallow pan or dish and pour the marinade over the meat, turning from time to time for 30 minutes to an hour.

To make the dipping sauce, heat the peanut oil in a small pot until nearly smoking, turn off the heat, and immediately add the peanuts. They should cook to a light golden in 3 to 5 minutes. Remove with a slotted spoon to a food processor or blender, along with a tablespoon of the cooking oil, reserving the rest. Grind to a rough paste, then add the chiles, ginger, and garlic, and continue to blend. Add the remaining ingredients, except the cilantro, and blend until smooth. Remove to a small mixing bowl and stir in the cilantro leaves along with half of the reserved oil or more. Transfer to appropriate dipping saucers.

Grill the satays about a minute per side—do not overcook—and serve with the dipping sauce.

(continued)

NOTE: To make tamarind paste, in a small pot cook half an 8-ounce package of tamarind pulp with 1 cup water until it softens. Pour the mixture into a strainer and rub the pulp through as best you can, leaving behind the seeds and strings of the pod. The result will be a brown paste, ¾ of a cup of which you'll need for the marinade.

Makes 32 1-ounce satays

Lamb Satays

○

Another popular satay that we serve regularly.

1 pound lamb flank

Sixteen 12-inch bamboo skewers

MARINADE

2 tablespoons bean sauce

2 tablespoons hoisin sauce

1 tablespoon light soy sauce

1 tablespoon dark soy sauce

1 tablespoon chili paste with garlic

1 tablespoon sugar

2 tablespoons sesame oil

2 tablespoons good peanut oil

¼ cup chopped fresh cilantro leaves

Peanut sauce for dipping (page 62)

Cut the lamb into 1-ounce slices of about 1 x 3 inches (you should get about 16 satays) and load them onto the bamboo skewers, leaving a generous handle. Mix the marinade ingredients thoroughly, and brush the lamb with this mixture.

Grill until medium-rare, brushing twice more during the grilling. Serve arranged on a platter sprinkled with the cilantro, with the dipping sauce on the side.

Chinese Barbecued Pork Shoulder

Called *cha siu*, these sweet, reddish glazed strips of roasted pork can be seen hanging in the windows of Chinatown markets next to roast ducks, soy braised chickens and other roast meats.

Once roasted, the pork strips can be eaten plainly, either warm or at room temperature (they're impossible to resist when they come out of the oven); or, the best plan is to make the quantity below, eat some of it, and wrap and store the rest to use in other dishes. This pork is excellent in noodle dishes and fried rice. The book calls for it three times: in lettuce packages (*soong*) (page 27); with Chow Fun rice noodles (page 107); or stir-fried with shrimp and peas (page 133).

3 pounds boneless pork shoulder (pork butt)

BARBECUE SAUCE

1 cup hoisin sauce

1 cup plum sauce (available in jars or cans in Chinese markets)

⅔ cups oyster sauce

2 teaspoons sugar

2 tablespoons dark soy sauce

2 tablespoons Shaoxing rice wine

2 tablespoons honey

1 tablespoon chili paste with garlic

1 tablespoon chopped garlic

1 tablespoon chopped ginger

Makes about 3 cups

Mix together the hoisin sauce, plum sauce, oyster sauce, sugar, soy sauce, rice wine, honey, chili paste, garlic, and ginger.

Cut the pork shoulder into 2-inch strips, about 6–8 inches in length. You'll get about 10 pieces. Marinate the strips for 1 hour in 1¾ cups of the barbecue sauce.

Preheat the oven to 550 degrees. Place the strips close together on a sheet pan. Put the sheet pan in the oven near the top and roast for 10 minutes. Turn the meat over and roast for another 10 minutes. Then keep on turning the meat every 10–12 minutes until it has roasted 45–50 minutes.

Remove from the oven and allow the pork to cool, turning the meat in the sauce as it cools so it will continue to glaze. To eat immediately, slice as many strips as you want thinly on a bias across the grain. Or, if you want to save some or all for another use, the cooled strips can be wrapped individually in foil and refrigerated. They'll keep up to a week.

To serve alone, sliced thinly as part of a larger meal, allow ½ strip per person.

We serve a variety of lettuce packages known as "soongs" at Big Bowl. They consist of a warm filling that is spooned into cool, crisp lettuce leaves, dabbed with a sauce, then wrapped and eaten. Originally a Southern Chinese dish, soong's traditional main ingredient is minced squab. Here are four of our favorites.

Thai Chicken Soong (Lettuce Packages)

2 tablespoons fish sauce

1 tablespoon sugar

2 tablespoons fresh lime juice

½ teaspoon kosher salt

¼ cup peanut or vegetable oil

¼ cup red onion, diced

2 tablespoons sliced scallion

2 tablespoons diced fresh red chile pepper

½ cup diced celery (¼ inch)

1 tablespoon chopped lemongrass

2 tablespoons peeled and diced fresh
　water chestnuts

¾ pound ground chicken leg meat

1 teaspoon cornstarch mixed with
　1 tablespoon water

½ teaspoon freshly ground black pepper

1 tablespoon chopped fresh Thai basil

1 tablespoon chopped fresh mint

2 tablespoons fresh whole cilantro leaves

1 kaffir lime leaf, julienned (optional)

8 to 10 crisp Bibb lettuce leaves

SAUCE

3½ tablespoons fresh lime juice

1 teaspoon minced fresh garlic

2 tablespoons sugar

¼ cup fish sauce

Mix together the fish sauce, sugar, lime juice, and salt, and set aside.

Heat a wok or skillet and add the peanut oil. When hot, add the onion, scallion, chiles, celery, lemongrass, and fresh water chestnuts and sauté, tossing over high heat for 30 seconds. Add the chicken and continue to cook until the meat changes color.

Stir in the fish sauce mixture and bring to a boil. Recombine the cornstarch and water and drizzle into the dish. Continue to stir until the mixture has a clear glaze. Remove from the heat, stir in the black pepper, basil, mint, cilantro, and kaffir lime leaf. Toss to combine and remove to a small decorative bowl. Place this on a larger platter or plate, and surround with crisp, shapely Bibb lettuce leaves.

Combine all the ingredients for the sauce and place in a small serving dish. Pass the sauce separately for the guests to help themselves.

Makes 10–12 lettuce packages

Chinese Vegetable Soong
(Lettuce Packages)

○

This traditional Chinese vegetable soong is a great vegetarian appetizer. It's our favorite version, and is increasingly served in Chinese-American restaurants. The hoisin-based sauce on the side should be familiar to anyone who has enjoyed not only these vegetable packages in restaurants but also mu shu pork or Beijing duck.

8 medium dried black mushrooms

¼ cup peanut oil

1 cup diced, spiced, pressed tofu
   (¼-inch dice)

1 cup diced bamboo shoots
   (¼-inch dice)

½ cup sliced scallions (green and white)

¾ cup diced celery

⅓ cup diced, peeled fresh water
   chestnuts

½ cup reserved mushroom soaking liquid

2 tablespoons oyster sauce or vegetarian
   oyster sauce

1 tablespoon light soy sauce

1 teaspoon sugar

¼ teaspoon kosher salt

1 teaspoon cornstarch dissolved in
   1 tablespoon water

½ teaspoon freshly ground black pepper

1 teaspoon sesame oil

8 to 10 crisp Bibb lettuce leaves

SAUCE

¼ cup hoisin sauce

1 tablespoon light soy sauce

1 teaspoon sesame oil

Cover the mushrooms in hot tap water and allow to sit at least 30 minutes. Squeeze out the moisture, cut off the stems, and cut into a ¼-inch dice.

Heat a wok or skillet and add the oil. When hot add the mushrooms, stir briefly. Add the tofu, bamboo shoots, scallions, celery, and water chestnuts, and sauté over high heat. Add the reserved mushroom soaking liquid, oyster sauce, soy sauce, sugar, and salt, and cook until the sauce boils. Dribble in the cornstarch mixture and cook until the wok ingredients develop a clear glaze, about 30 seconds. Remove from the heat, stir in the black pepper, and drizzle with the sesame oil. Toss to combine and remove to a small decorative bowl. Surround with crisp, shapely Bibb lettuce leaves. Combine the ingredients for the sauce with 1 tablespoon water and pass it separately.

Makes 8–10 lettuce packages

Burmese Red Curry Pork Soong
(Lettuce Packages)

○

Unique to Big Bowl, this soong is made with pork and imbued with the flavors of toasted curry spices and fresh herbs.

1 tablespoon fish sauce

1 teaspoon sugar

1 tablespoon fresh lime juice

¼ teaspoon kosher salt

¼ cup peanut or vegetable oil

¾ pound fatty pork, ground once

2 tablespoons red curry paste

¼ cup diced red onion

2 tablespoons diced fresh red chile pepper

½ cup diced celery (¼-inch dice)

1 tablespoon chopped lemongrass

¼ cup chopped fresh water chestnuts

¼ cup chicken stock

1 teaspoon cornstarch dissolved in 1 tablespoon water

2 teaspoons ground dried shrimp

1 tablespoon ground roasted unsalted peanuts

½ teaspoon freshly ground black pepper

1 tablespoon chopped fresh Thai basil

1 tablespoon chopped fresh mint

2 tablespoons whole fresh cilantro leaves

8 to 10 crisp Bibb lettuce leaves

SAUCE

3½ tablespoons fresh lime juice

1 teaspoon minced fresh red chiles, seeds and all

2 tablespoons sugar

¼ cup fish sauce

Mix together the fish sauce, sugar, lime juice, and salt, and set aside.

Heat a wok or skillet and add the peanut oil. When hot add the pork and cook stirring and mashing to separate the pieces, just until the pork changes color. Stir in the curry paste and continue to cook, stirring. Add the onion, chiles, celery, lemongrass, and fresh water chestnuts and sauté, tossing, over high heat for 30 seconds. Add the chicken stock and continue to cook until it boils.

Stir in the fish sauce mixture and bring to a boil again. Dribble in the cornstarch mixture and cook until the wok ingredients develop a clear glaze, about 30 seconds. Remove from the heat, stir in the dried shrimp, peanuts, black pepper, basil, mint, and cilantro. Toss to combine and remove to a small decorative bowl. Surround with crisp, shapely Bibb lettuce leaves. Combine the sauce ingredients and pass separately.

Makes 10–12 lettuce packages

Chinese Barbecued Pork Soong
(Lettuce Packages)

○

This is a wonderful use for Chinese Barbecued Pork Shoulder (see page 23). The combination of the crisp lettuce leaves, the sweet glazed pork, the celery, and the oyster sauce creates the best kind of what we might call a Chinese-American restaurant flavor.

6 dried black mushrooms

SAUCE

¼ cup hoisin sauce

1 tablespoon light soy sauce

1 tablespoon water

1 teaspoon sesame oil

¾ pound of barbecued pork,
    cut into a ¼-inch dice

3 tablespoons of peanut oil

¼ cup peanut or vegetable oil

½ cup diced bamboo shoots

½ cup thinly sliced scallions

½ cup chopped celery

3 tablespoons peeled and diced
    fresh water chestnuts

2 tablespoons oyster sauce

2 teaspoons light soy sauce

1½ teaspoons sugar

¼ teaspoon kosher salt

½ cup chicken stock

1½ teaspoons cornstarch dissolved
    in 1½ tablespoons water

½ teaspoon freshly ground
    black pepper

½ teaspoon sesame oil

8–10 crisp bibb lettuce leaves

Cover the mushrooms with hot tap water and let them soak at least 30 minutes. Squeeze out the moisture, discard the liquid, cut off and discard the stems, and cut into a ¼-inch dice.

Combine the sauce ingredients.

Heat a wok or skillet over high heat and add the oil. When hot, add the mushrooms; stir briefly. Add the pork and stir briefly, just to coat with the oil. Add the bamboo shoots, scallions, celery, and water chestnuts, and sauté for 1 minute. Add the chicken stock, oyster sauce, soy sauce, sugar, and salt, and cook until the sauce boils. Dribble in the cornstarch mixture and cook until the mixture develops a clear glaze, about 30 seconds.

Remove from the heat, stir in the black pepper, and drizzle with the sesame oil. Toss to combine and remove to a small decorative bowl. Surround with crisp, shapely Bibb lettuce leaves. Pass the sauce separately.

Serves 3 to 4 as an appetizer

27

Dumplings, little meat or vegetable-filled pouches of dough, have long been popular in China. Big Bowl's most popular appetizer for example, is the Northern Chinese "potsticker," and we sell several varieties of the soft, succulent, boiled wonton. Here are two kinds: the first, Green Vegetable Wontons, is a menu item at Big Bowl and is used in a menu item soup (page 66); the second, Salmon Dumplings with Coconut Curry Sauce (page 30), is a special event dish. Both require store-bought fresh wonton skins.

Green Vegetable "Steamer Basket" Wontons with Chinese Chives and Mustard Greens
(Gai Choy)

○

This traditional Eastern Chinese green vegetable stuffing, which includes Chinese chives, mustard greens, and peanuts, is wrapped in wonton skins and served two ways: with a dip sauce (in little steamer baskets), or as the feature item in a soup with noodles.

1 tablespoon plus 1 teaspoon kosher salt

1 pound spinach leaves, cleaned

1 pound mustard greens (gai choy)

½ pound Chinese chives

1 bunch fresh cilantro, leaves and stems

3 ounces bamboo shoots, chopped

3 tablespoons chopped carrots

2 tablespoons chopped, soaked dried shiitake mushrooms

1 cup chopped, fried peanuts

2 tablespoons sesame oil

3 tablespoons peanut oil

3 tablespoons cornstarch

1½ tablespoons sugar

2 tablespoons light soy sauce

One 1-pound package fresh, thin wonton skins

Sprinkle 1 tablespoon salt over the spinach, *gai choy*, chives, cilantro, bamboo, and carrots; toss and let stand 30 minutes. Bring some water in the bottom of a large, covered steamer to boil. Put the vegetables in a heatproof bowl that will fit inside the steamer and steam, covered, for 2 minutes or until wilted. Wrap the vegetables in cheesecloth or in a clean kitchen towel and squeeze out the moisture. Chop them coarsely (do not mince). Add the shiitake, peanuts, both oils, cornstarch, sugar, light soy sauce, and remaining teaspoon of salt, and mix well.

SAUCE

1 tablespoon chopped ginger

1 tablespoon chopped garlic

¼ cup light soy sauce

¼ cup rice wine vinegar

1 tablespoon sugar

1 tablespoon sesame oil

Spread a wonton skin in front of you. Place 1 teaspoon of the filling in the center of the skin. Dampen the edges of skin with water and fold in half, pressing the edges to seal. Then with the folded edge facing you, pull the bottom corners directly down, fold them over one another slightly, and pinch to seal. The resulting dumpling should look like a nurse's cap. Repeat until filling has been used.

Combine the sauce ingredients.

Bring a large quantity of water to a boil. When rapidly boiling, add the wontons (not so much that the water will stop boiling, about 20), and cook for 3 to 4 minutes or until opaque. Remove, drain, and serve in individual bowls sprinkled with a small quantity of the sauce.

NOTE: At Big Bowl we serve these in soup (after boiling) with seasoned chicken or vegetable broth, some cooked Shanghai noodles, a few slices of shiitake and spinach. The soup is sprinkled with black pepper and sesame oil before serving. (See All-Vegetable Wonton Soup, page 66.)

You may serve these simply in seasoned chicken broth with some spinach for color.

Makes 60 to 80 wontons; serves 8 to 10

Salmon Dumplings
with Coconut Curry Sauce

○

This popular appetizer we reserve for special occasions. The beauty of these is that all the tender morsels of the fish that are left behind when the fish is filleted can be put to delicious use in this filling. These dumplings are rich and delicious.

4 ounces fresh pork fat

1 pound salmon, preferably wild

1 teaspoon sesame oil

1 teaspoon finely minced ginger

1 tablespoon finely sliced scallion

1 teaspoon fish sauce

¼ cup chopped fresh cilantro leaves

1 tablespoon peanut oil

1 teaspoon kosher salt

¼ teaspoon sugar

½ egg white, beaten

1 teaspoon cornstarch

1½ tablespoons chicken stock

½ teaspoon black pepper

30 to 40 fresh wonton skins

Simmer the pork fat in water to cover for 15 minutes. Drain, allow to cool, and chop finely.

Cut the salmon into a small dice. Put all the ingredients, except the wonton skins, into a mixing bowl and stir in one direction until mixed.

Spread a wonton skin in front of you. Put 1 teaspoon of the filling in the center of the skin. Dampen the edges of the skin with water and fold in half, pressing the edges to seal. Then, with the folded edge facing you, pull the bottom corners directly down, fold them over one another slightly, and pinch to seal. The resulting dumpling should look like a nurse's cap. Repeat until filling has been used.

Bring a large quantity of water to a boil. When rapidly boiling, add the wontons (not so much that the water will stop boiling, about half), and cook for 3 to 4 minutes or until opaque. Remove, drain, and serve over or with the Coconut Curry Sauce (page 30):

NOTE: The wontons can be made up to a day ahead and kept refrigerated, lightly covered on a sheet tray. In a pinch they can be frozen and added to the boiling water frozen. (They'll take slightly longer to cook.)

Makes 30 to 40 dumplings; 6 to 8 servings

Coconut Curry Sauce for Salmon Dumplings

2 tablespoons fresh Yellow Curry
   Paste (page 16)

One 14-ounce can unsweetened
   coconut milk, preferably
   Chaokoh brand

½ cup chicken stock

1 tablespoon fish sauce

Juice of 1 lime

¼ cup lightly chopped cilantro leaves

Heat a saucepan and add the curry paste.
Sauté very briefly. Add the coconut milk and
chicken stock, and simmer until the sauce
reduces by one-third. Set aside.

While boiling the dumplings, reheat the
coconut milk mixture; add the fish sauce and
lime juice and, when the dumplings are done,
drizzle the sauce generously over a serving
plate. Sprinkle with the fresh cilantro. Arrange
the dumplings over the sauce and serve.

NOTE: You may also stir the cilantro into the sauce and serve it on the side, allowing each diner to help herself.

Makes about 1½ cups

Pearl Balls

○

These dim sum–style inviting little morsels first appeared in Chinese-American restaurants decades ago and then disappeared. Presented best in a bamboo steamer basket lined with banana leaves, they are golf ball–sized spheres of seasoned, chopped chicken and shrimp covered with a coating of sticky rice, and then steamed. It's worth investing in a bamboo steamer basket and banana leaves to line it with, to present this dish properly. Banana leaves can be purchased fresh or frozen in Southeast Asian markets.

2 cups Chinese glutinous rice ("sticky rice")

¾ pound chicken thigh meat, ground or chopped

½ pound shrimp, peeled, deveined, and chopped

¼ cup chicken stock

2 dried black mushrooms, soaked, drained, stems removed, and cut into small dice

¼ cup chopped bamboo shoots

½ cup sliced scallion greens

2 fresh water chestnuts, peeled and chopped

2 teaspoons finely minced ginger

¼ cup lightly chopped fresh cilantro leaves

2 tablespoons light soy sauce

1 teaspoon sugar

1 teaspoon kosher salt

1 teaspoon freshly ground black pepper

1 tablespoon sesame oil

PEARL BALL DIP SAUCE MIXTURE
(to be made before cooking)

¼ cup red wine vinegar

5 tablespoon light soy sauce

1 ½ tablespoons sugar

1 tablespoon chopped garlic

1 tablespoon green scallion, thinly sliced

2 teaspoons sesame oil

Soak the rice for 8 hours or overnight in cold water to cover. When soaked, drain away the water and rinse the rice in a change or two of water. Drain and spread the rice evenly over a plate.

Put the remaining ingredients, except the sauce components, into a mixing bowl and stir in one direction until well mixed (this aerates the mixture, rendering it more tender). Moistening your hands from time to time with a little water, form the filling into 1-ounce balls. Press each ball into the rice to coat, and arrange in a steamer section until ready to cook. You may need two steamer sections to hold all the pearl balls.

In a covered steamer bring a large quantity of water to a boil. Insert the section or sections with the pearl balls and steam for 15 to 20 minutes, until the rice is translucent. Serve in the steamer basket or on a platter with the dip sauce divided among individual saucers.

Makes 20 balls, serves 4 to 6 as part of a larger meal

Most soups at Big Bowl are meal-in-a-bowl. The three soups that follow are for people to share or eat individually to start a meal. Chinese Hot and Sour Soup can also serve as a main course.

Velvet Corn Soup with Ham

When summer corn is at its peak, we offer this dish. It's best to shuck the corn right into the broth, tossing in salt to draw out the delicious fresh corn flavor. Stirring in the egg whites is a little tricky, but, if done correctly, they'll look like clouds. The soup is quickly prepared.

4 ears of freshly picked sweet corn

3 cups chicken stock

1 ½ teaspoons salt

2 teaspoons cornstarch mixed with 2 tablespoons water

3 egg whites lightly beaten with 1 teaspoon half-and-half and ½ teaspoon sesame oil

2 tablespoons finely chopped Smithfield ham

Husk and shuck the corn into a bowl along with any milky liquid you can wring out of the ears.

Heat the stock to boiling, add the salt and corn, and allow the mixture to come to a boil. Give the cornstarch-water mixture another stir and add to the soup. When the soup is beginning to boil again, and has thickened slightly and is clear, turn the heat to medium and stir the soup in one direction slowly with a spoon. With your other hand, pour the egg whites into the broth in a thin stream. When the egg is set, transfer the soup to serving bowls, sprinkle with the ham, and serve.

Makes 3 to 4 small servings

Steamed Mussels
in Coconut Herb Broth

○

This tasty shellfish soup produces an irresistibly aromatic broth. It's meant as a prelude to a meal.

1 teaspoon peanut oil

6 thin slices galangal

1 lemongrass stalk, bottom 3 inches sliced thinly on a bias

1 serrano chile, julienned (seeds and all)

1 kaffir lime leaf (optional)

15 mussels, debearded and scrubbed (about ½ pound)

1 cup chicken broth

1 teaspoon fish sauce

1 teaspoon sugar

2 tablespoons coconut milk

2 Thai basil leaves, julienned

1 tablespoon fresh cilantro leaves

¼ small lime

Healthy dash of freshly ground black pepper

Heat a large saucepan or skillet. Add the oil. When hot, add the galangal, lemongrass, chile pepper, and lime leaf, and stir briefly. Add the mussels and toss briefly with the herbs. Add the chicken broth and simmer until the mussels open. Discard any that don't open. Stir in the fish sauce, sugar, and coconut milk, bring to a boil, and immediately turn off the heat.

Pour the broth into one or two serving bowls (holding back the mussels). Sprinkle in the basil and cilantro leaves, squeeze in the lime, add the pepper, then arrange the mussels in the bowl(s) on top. Serve.

Makes 2 to 3 small servings

Chinese Hot and Sour Soup

○

This classic Northern Chinese soup became popular in the United States in the late 1960s. While full of exotic flavors and textures and peppery hot, it's essentially an ages-old doctor's prescription straight from the Chinese *materia medica*. That old elixir, chicken soup, is the medium for day lily buds and tree ear and shiitake mushrooms, all thought to be good for the circulation; protein from tofu, pork, and egg; and the cooling antiseptic properties of vinegar balanced by the heat of freshly ground white pepper—the "hot" in Hot and Sour Soup. A steam table soup at most Chinese restaurants, try it here fresh, the way we make it at Big Bowl.

1/3 cup pork loin, julienned

1½ teaspoons dark soy sauce

12 dried day lily buds, soaked, trimmed, and pulled into shreds by hand (see Note)

2 dried black mushrooms

8 small dried tree ear mushrooms

2 tablespoons red wine vinegar

1½ teaspoons light soy sauce

1 teaspoon kosher salt

½ teaspoon sugar

1 tablespoon peanut oil

1/3 cup tofu, julienned

¼ cup bamboo shoots, julienned

2 cups chicken broth

1 egg, slightly beaten with a few drops of sesame oil

1 tablespoon cornstarch mixed with 2 tablespoons water

½ teaspoon sesame oil

½ teaspoon freshly ground white pepper

1 tablespoon thinly sliced scallion greens

1 tablespoon cilantro leaves

Mix the pork with the dark soy sauce and set aside. Soak and shred the lily buds and set aside. Pour hot water over the dried mushrooms and tree ears, and let them soak 30 minutes.

Combine the vinegar, light soy sauce, salt, and sugar, and set aside.

When the mushrooms have soaked, remove from the soaking liquid, discarding it. Cut off the hard stems, and slice the mushrooms across the caps. Simply remove and drain the tree ears.

Heat a wok or small heavy pot over high heat. Add the oil and, when hot, add the pork. Sauté quickly, separating the shreds, until the meat changes color. Add the mushrooms, tree ears, bamboo shoots, and lily buds. Sauté briefly.

Add the broth and bring to a boil. Add the tofu and, when the broth boils, add the seasonings. Recombine the cornstarch and water mixture and add to the boiling broth. Turn the heat down and, stirring the soup slowly in one direction with a spoon, pour in the beaten egg in a thin stream. Transfer to a serving vessel. Drizzle with the sesame oil. Sprinkle on the pepper. Add the scallions and cilantro and serve.

NOTE: Lily buds, sometimes called "golden needles," are available dried, but still slightly soft, in 8-ounce plastic packages in Chinese markets. They should be soaked in warm water to cover until soft. The hard tips should be cut off and each bud should be pulled apart lengthwise once or twice by hand before being added to the soup.

Serves 2 as part of a larger meal

S eafood small plates are very popular. Here are three special seafood appetizers that are highly recommended.

Pan-Roasted Shrimp-Stuffed Chile Peppers

○

E legant and delicious with a roasted pepper flavor, this red pepper appetizer is offered regularly at Big Bowl. Here the peppers are stuffed with shrimp and fish; we occasionally make a version with fresh lump crabmeat as well. Serve as a first course or as part of a meal.

15 to 20 medium, fresh red chile peppers, 2–2½ inches long (we use fresnos; cayenne will do)

Cornstarch

STUFFING

¾ pound shrimp, peeled, deveined, and chopped

¼ pound fresh white-fleshed fish such as halibut, chopped

½ pound fatty pork such as fresh, uncured bacon, ground

¼ cup finely chopped fresh water chestnuts

½ cup thinly sliced scallion greens

1 teaspoon finely minced ginger

1 ½ teaspoons kosher salt

1 ½ tablespoons cornstarch

2 egg whites

2 tablespoons white wine

2 tablespoons sesame oil

Cut the chiles in half lengthwise, remove the seeds, and dust the inside of each chile half lightly with cornstarch. Add the shrimp, fish, pork, water chestnuts, scallion, ginger, salt, cornstarch, egg whites, wine, and sesame oil to a mixing bowl and stir with your fingers in one direction to mix.

Stuff each chile half with the shrimp mixture—the stuffing should come just above the edge of the chile. When done, prepare the sauce.

Mix together the chicken broth, oyster sauce, soy sauce, salt, and sugar and set aside. Heat to medium-hot a skillet large enough to cook 20 shrimp-stuffed chile halves. When hot, add the peanut oil. To the hot oil, add the chiles filling side down. Cook over medium heat for 1 minute or until golden brown. (The pan shouldn't be too hot, or the shrimp mixture will burn.)

SAUCE FOR PAN-COOKED CHILES
(for a batch of 20 halves)

1 ½ cups chicken broth

2 tablespoons oyster sauce

2 tablespoons light soy sauce

½ teaspoon salt

1½ teaspoons sugar

¼ cup peanut oil

1 tablespoon salted black beans

1 tablespoon finely chopped ginger

1 tablespoon finely chopped garlic

Coriander sprigs for garnish

Turn the chiles over and allow the pepper side to cook for 1 minute or so, or until they brown slightly. Push the peppers together to give yourself a little room in the pan to add the black beans, ginger, and garlic. Sauté these seasonings briefly, then add the seasoned stock by pouring it around the pan. Cover and cook for another 1½ minutes.

Uncover, check for doneness (they should feel firm), remove to a serving platter, and keep warm. Turn the heat under the sauce to high and cook until slightly thickened.

Pour over the chiles and serve garnished with sprigs of cilantro.

Makes 15 to 20 stuffed chiles

Pan-Seared and Braised Flower Mushrooms Stuffed with Shrimp

○

These mushrooms make a visually arresting first course. The caps are stuffed with a tasty mixture of shrimp and fresh fish that is complemented by a little fresh pork.

25 dried black "flower" mushrooms,
     1½ inches in diameter (see Note)

Cornstarch

STUFFING

¾ pound shrimp, peeled, deveined,
     and chopped

¼ pound fresh white-fleshed fish,
     such as halibut, chopped

½ pound fatty ground pork,
     such as fresh, uncured bacon

¼ cup finely chopped fresh water
     chestnuts

½ cup thinly sliced scallion greens

1 teaspoon finely minced ginger

1½ teaspoons kosher salt

1½ tablespoons cornstarch

2 egg whites

2 tablespoons Shaoxing rice wine

2 tablespoons sesame oil

Put the mushrooms in a bowl and cover them with 2 cups of hot tap water. Let them soak for 2 hours. When soaked, remove the mushrooms from the bowl and squeeze them back into the bowl, reserving the liquid. Cut out the stems of the mushrooms and dust the inside of the caps lightly with cornstarch.

Add all the stuffing ingredients to a mixing bowl and stir with your fingers in one direction to mix.

Stuff each mushroom with the shrimp mixture—the stuffing should be slightly rounded above the edge of the mushroom.

To make the sauce, mix together the mushroom liquid, oyster sauce, soy sauce, salt, and sugar. Heat a skillet large enough to cook 25 shrimp-stuffed mushrooms over medium-high heat (this may be done in 2 batches). When hot, add the peanut oil. Add the mushrooms, filling-side down, to the hot oil. Cook over medium heat for 1 minute or until golden brown. (The pan shouldn't be too hot or the shrimp mixture will burn.)

SAUCE FOR PAN-SEARED MUSHROOMS
(FOR A BATCH OF 25)

1½ cups reserved mushroom soaking liquid

2 tablespoons oyster sauce

2 tablespoons light soy sauce

½ teaspoon salt

1½ teaspoons sugar

¼ cup peanut oil

1 tablespoon ginger, finely chopped

1 tablespoon garlic, finely chopped

coriander sprigs for garnish

Turn the mushrooms over and cook the cap side for 1 minute or so, or until they brown slightly. Push the mushrooms together to create room in the pan for thr ginger and garlic. Sauté these seasonings briefly, then pour the seasoned stock around the pan. Cover and cook for another 1½ minutes.

Uncover, check the mushrooms for doneness (they should still feel firm), and remove to a serving platter and keep warm. Turn the heat under the sauce to high and cook until slightly thickened.

Pour over the mushrooms and serve garnished with sprigs of fresh coriander.

NOTE: Although any dried black mushroom 1½ inches in diameter that you find at a Chinese grocery will do, the best are the thick-capped variety that is laced with white fissures, sometimes called "flower mushrooms." They are most easily found at Chinese herbal shops; their cost is well worth it.

Serves 4 to 6 as part of a large meal, 8 or more as an appetizer

Big Bowl Crab Cakes

○

A Thai twist to the all-American crab cake, wonderfully fragrant herbs such as lemongrass, ginger, and Thai basil add compelling refinement to this popular appetizer.

COCONUT BASIL SAUCE FOR CRAB CAKES

One 14-ounce can unsweetened coconut milk, preferably Chaokoh brand

½ cup chicken stock

2 tablespoons fish sauce

Juice of 1 lime

1 teaspoon finely minced lemongrass

¾ pound fresh back fin crabmeat

½ pound fresh Alaskan halibut, chopped

¼ pound shrimp, peeled, deveined, and chopped

¼ pound pork fat

2 teapoons cornstarch

¼ cup Japanese bread crumbs

3 egg whites

½ tablespoon finely minced ginger

½ tablespoon finely minced lemongrass

½ teaspoon black pepper

2 teaspoons fish sauce

1½ teaspoons kosher salt

6 tablespoons minced red onion

¼ cup sliced scallion green

¼ cup fresh cilantro leaves, lightly chopped

2 tablespoons Thai basil leaves, lightly chopped, plus a pinch for garnish

2 tablespoons chopped fresh cilantro leaves

Freshly ground black pepper

Begin the sauce ahead of time. In a saucepan, simmer the coconut milk and chicken stock together until they reduce by one third.

Break the crabmeat up lightly and set it aside. Place the halibut and shrimp in a separate mixing bowl. Blanch the pork fat in a small saucepan of simmering water for 10 minutes. Remove when cool; chop as finely as possible. Add to the halibut-shrimp mixture along with the cornstarch, bread crumbs, egg whites, ginger, lemongrass, black pepper, fish sauce, salt, onion, scallion, cilantro, and lightly chopped basil, and stir with your fingers in one direction to mix. Fold in the crabmeat, taking care that it doesn't break up too much.

With your hands, form the mixture into cakes of about 2 inches in diameter, 2 ounces each (you'll have about 15). In a lightly oiled skillet over medium heat, cook the cakes on each side until golden brown and cooked through, 2 to 3 minutes on a side.

While the crab cakes are cooking (or when they're just done), continue making the sauce. Reheat the coconut milk mixture and add the fish sauce, lime juice, and lemongrass. Drizzle the sauce generously over a serving plate. Sprinkle with the chopped fresh herbs. Arrange the crab cakes, sprinkle with the black pepper, and serve.

NOTE: You may also stir the chopped herbs into the sauce and serve it and the pepper on the side, allowing each diner to help herself.

Makes about 15 crab cakes

Golden Shrimp Toast with Sesame Seeds

Light and juicy and with wonderful shrimp flavor that is complemented by the subtle sweet crunch of fresh water chestnuts, this is one of the all-time great appetizers.

½ pound fresh peeled, deveined shrimp

3 ounces fresh pork fat

2 egg whites

3 teaspoons cornstarch

¾ teaspoon kosher salt

1 teaspoon finely minced, peeled ginger

¼ cup finely chopped fresh water chestnuts

3 teaspoons Shaoxing rice wine

1 teaspoon sesame oil

2 tablespoons water or chicken stock

2 egg yolks

8 thin slices dense white bread (e.g., Old-Fashioned Pepperidge Farm—not bread labeled "thin-sliced"—it's too thin)

1 cup white sesame seeds

Oil for frying

Chop shrimp by hand with a cleaver or French chef's knife.

Simmer the pork fat in a saucepan with water for 15 minutes, allow to cool and finely chop.

In a mixing bowl stir the shrimp and fat together in one direction with the egg whites, 1½ teaspoons cornstarch, salt, ginger, 1 teaspoon wine, sesame oil, and water (or stock). Mix the egg yolks to a paste with the remaining 1½ teaspoons cornstarch and the remaining Shaoxing wine.

Stack the bread and cut the crusts away, leaving slices about 2½ inches square. With a pastry brush, paint one side of each slice with the egg yolk/cornstarch/wine paste.

Turn the bread over and, with a rubber spatula, spread about ¼ inch of the shrimp mixture evenly over the top. Pour the sesame seeds into a small plate and lightly press the shrimp side of the bread into the sesame seeds to cover the top. Put the bread, yellow side down, on wax paper until ready to cook (up to 3 hours, unrefrigerated).

In a large wok or large, deep skillet, bring 6 cups of oil to 360 degrees.

Place the bread, a few slices at a time, shrimp side down, in the oil, and cook for about 1 minute; turn and cook until the entire bottom is light golden. Turn again and cook for another 30 seconds until the shrimp mixture puffs up slightly. Remove to drain on paper towels. (Once you're experienced, you may cook as many as your frying surface will fit comfortably.)

Allow to cool slightly and cut into three "sticks"; serve arranged on a serving platter.

Makes 24 finger-sized sticks of shrimp toast

Spring Rolls Stuffed
with Fresh Crabmeat and Shrimp

○

Created by Big Bowl chef trainer Raul Gutierrez, they use the same stuffing as the Big Bowl crab cakes (see page 40), and are the best possible appetizers for passing around.

see page 40

STUFFING

¾ pound fresh back fin crabmeat

½ pound fresh Alaskan halibut, chopped

¼ pound shrimp, peeled, deveined, and chopped

¼ pound pork fat

2 teapoons cornstarch

¼ cup Japanese bread crumbs

3 egg whites

½ tablespoon finely minced ginger

½ tablespoon finely minced lemongrass

½ teaspoon black pepper

2 teaspoons fish sauce

1½ teaspoons kosher salt

6 tablespoons minced red onion

¼ cup sliced scallion green

¼ cup cilantro leaves, lightly chopped

¼ cup Thai basil leaves, lightly chopped

1 package (25 sheets) spring roll wrappers (see Note on page 44)

2 egg whites, lightly beaten

see Note on page 44

SAUCE

1 tablespoon chopped ginger

1 tablespoon chopped garlic

¼ cup light soy sauce

¼ cup rice wine vinegar

1 tablespoon sugar

1 tablespoon sesame oil

To make the stuffing, break the crabmeat up lightly and set it aside. Place the halibut and shrimp in a separate mixing bowl. Blanch the pork fat in a small saucepan of simmering water for 10 minutes. Remove and, when cool, chop it as finely as possible. Add to the seafood along with the remaining ingredients and stir with your fingers in one direction to mix. Fold in the crabmeat taking care that it doesn't break up too much.

To make the spring rolls, place one spring roll wrapper in front of you with the bottom edge parallel to your worktable. Scoop about 3 tablespoons of the crabmeat mixture (1½ ounces) and spread it across the entire length of the spring roll wrapper, about 1 inch from the bottom. Using a pastry brush, paint the side and top edges of the wrapper above the filling with the egg white. Roll up the spring roll straight and tight as you would a cigar, leaving the ends open (they'll seal naturally when cooked). Repeat until they are all rolled. You should have 20 spring rolls. Mix the ingredients for the dipping sauce.

Fry the spring rolls a few at a time in 375-degree oil (you may use a wok for this). Remove and drain on paper towels. When ready to serve, cut each roll on the bias into 3 pieces. Serve with the dipping sauce in strategically placed little saucers.

Makes about 20 spring rolls

Vietnamese Lemongrass-Chicken
Summer Rolls

Rice paper sheets, transparent and round, are fundamental to Vietnamese cooking. Used primarily as wrappers, they account for a near-infinite variety of wonderful little packages of food. Some, called "spring rolls," are stuffed and fried. The version here, essentially a Thai chicken salad wrapped in a soft, white, soaked sheet of this dough, is called a "summer roll."

2 pounds boneless chicken breast

2 tablespoons kosher salt

DRESSING

¼ cup fish sauce

3 tablespoons freshly squeezed lime juice

2 teaspoons sugar

1 tablespoon sesame oil

1 tablespoon peanut oil

2 tablespoons fine julienned fresh ginger

2 tablespoons fine julienned fresh red chile pepper

½ cup julienned, peeled, and seeded cucumbers

¼ cup julienned scallions

¼ cup julienned Thai basil leaves

¼ cup julienned fresh mint leaves

¼ cup cilantro leaves

1½ tablespoons finely chopped lemongrass

6 tablespoons chopped roasted peanuts

2 tablespoons finely chopped dried shrimp

⅓ cup minced red onion

1 12-ounce package Thai or Vietnamese rice paper wrappers (8½-inch rounds, see Note)

14 large Bibb lettuce leaves

Sprinkle the chicken breasts with the salt and let them sit for 20 minutes. Meanwhile mix together the sauce ingredients, first mixing the fish sauce, lime juice, and sugar together until the sugar dissolves.

Bring a pot of water to boil large enough to cover the chicken breasts. When boiling, add the chicken and bring to a boil again. Immediately turn off the heat, cover, and allow to sit for 20 minutes. Remove from the water—they should be not at all pink inside—and, with your hands, pull the chicken apart into shreds of about ¼ inch x 2 inches.

Put the chicken in a mixing bowl and add the ginger, chile pepper, cucumber, scallion, basil, mint, cilantro, lemongrass, peanuts, dried shrimp, and red onion. Add the dressing, including the sesame and peanut oils, and toss to mix.

Fill a bowl or shallow pan, large enough to dip a sheet of rice paper, with hot tap water.

Dip the rice paper sheets, one sheet at a time, into the hot water. When the sheet begins to soften, pull it out of the water, allow it to drain for a few seconds, and spread it in front of you on a cutting board.

(continued)

Put 1 Bibb lettuce leaf on top of the rice paper and spread ⅓ cup of the salad mixture on top of that, extending the width of the roll, 1½ inches below the midpoint of the wrapper. Then, taking the rice paper from the bottom, fold it tightly over the filling and continue rolling up as tightly as you can, leaving the ends of the roll open. The lettuce leaf helps to keep it tight and enhances the texture of the salad.

To serve, cut each roll into 2 or 3 pieces on the bias.

NOTE: Rice paper, called *banh trang* or sometimes "spring rolls skin," comes in round 12-ounce packages. The packages are of heavy clear plastic and hold about 25 of these paper-thin sheets.

Makes about 14 summer rolls, which would serve 6 to 10 as part of an appetizer selection

In the 1960s mu shu pork (along with Chinese Hot and Sour Soup [page 34], another Northern Chinese specialty) became a staple of Chinese-American menus. We serve a variety of these ancient wraps, but as a small-plate prelude to a meal. Here are two mu shu "wraps"; the second, with lamb, is the more traditional.

Thai Basil Mu Shu Wrap

○

Not native to Thailand, this dish is a popular takeoff on the Northern Chinese idea of wrapping ingredients in a tortilla-like pancake, sprinkling it with a sauce, rolling it, and enjoying it. This one is peppery and redolent with good Thai flavors such as dried shrimp, peanuts, and fish sauce.

SAUCE

1 tablespoon fish sauce

2 teaspoons lemon juice

1 teaspoon sugar

¼ pound chicken breast, julienned

1 teaspoon light soy sauce

1 teaspoon cornstarch

A few drops sesame oil

1 tablespoon fish sauce

2 teaspoons fresh lemon juice

1½ teaspoons sugar

¼ cup peanut oil

1 egg, lightly beaten

4 garlic cloves, minced

¼ cup julienned fresh red chile peppers

¼ cup julienned scallion

¼ cup julienned bamboo shoots

1 tablespoon chopped roasted peanuts

1 tablespoon dried shrimp powder (large dried shrimp ground in a food processor or spice grinder)

6 basil leaves, julienned

⅓ cup bean sprouts

6 Beijing pancakes, thawed if frozen (also called mu shu wrappers; we use the widely distributed brand Wei Chuen, which comes in 8-ounce packages and may be purchased at any Chinese grocery.)

Combine the sauce ingredients and set aside.

Toss the chicken shreds with the soy sauce, cornstarch, and sesame oil, and set aside.

Mix the fish sauce, lemon juice, and sugar; reserve.

Heat a wok or skillet until very hot. Add the peanut oil. When nearly smoking, add the egg and stir quickly to set. Push off to the side of the pan and add the chicken shreds. Stir quickly to separate the pieces. Then add the garlic, chile peppers, scallion, and bamboo shoots, and stir rapidly to coat with the oil. Add the fish sauce mixture and cook, tossing for 1 minute or so, or until the vegetables soften slightly. Toss in the peanuts and shrimp powder, then stir in the basil leaves. Pull the pan off the heat and add the bean sprouts. Toss until well mixed.

Meanwhile separate 6 to 8 of the pancakes and steam them briefly, wrapped together, in aluminum foil. Serve the hot Thai basil dish with the pancakes and sauce on the side for each guest to help herself.

Loin of Lamb Mu Shu Wrap

○

It's not mu shu pork, but it's close and just as authentically Northern Chinese. This is one of several dishes to be wrapped in traditional wheat flour pancakes that we serve at Big Bowl.

SAUCE

¼ cup hoisin sauce

2 teaspoons light soy sauce

1 teaspoon sugar

2 teaspoons sesame oil

2 large dried black mushrooms

1 tablespoon small dried cloud ear mushrooms

6 ounces loin of lamb, julienned

2 teaspoons dark Chinese soy sauce

1½ teaspoons sesame oil

1 teaspoon salt

1 teaspoon sugar

2 tablespoons Shaoxing rice wine

¼ cup peanut oil

1 egg, lightly beaten

⅓ cup julienned bamboo shoots

½ cup julienned scallions

½ cup sliced napa cabbage

¾ cup bean sprouts

½ teaspoon freshly ground white pepper

6 Beijing pancakes, thawed if frozen (also called "mu shu wrappers," we use the widely distributed brand Wei Chuen, which comes in 8-ounce packages and may be purchased at any Chinese grocery)

Combine the sauce ingredients and set aside.

Put the black mushrooms and the cloud ears in separate bowls, cover each with hot water, and let soak for 30 minutes. When the black mushrooms are soft, squeeze out the liquid, cut off the stems, and discard them. Slice them thinly. Drain and dry the cloud ears.

Mix the lamb shreds with 1½ teaspoons dark soy sauce and 1 teaspoon of the sesame oil and set aside.

Mix the salt and sugar with the rice wine and set aside.

Heat a wok or skillet. When smoking hot add the peanut oil. Add the egg to the hot oil and beat quickly to set. Push the eggs to the side of the pan. Add the lamb and cook, stirring to separate the shreds. Add the mushrooms and cook, stirring briefly, then the bamboo shoots, scallions, and napa cabbage, and drizzle over remaining ½ teaspoon dark soy sauce. Cook over high heat, stirring until the vegetables soften slightly, about 2 minutes.

Add the seasoned rice wine and continue to stir. Pull off the heat, stir in the bean sprouts, sprinkle with the pepper and remaining sesame oil, and leave in the pan.

Separate 6 to 8 of the pancakes, wrap together in aluminum foil, and steam them until hot, 30 seconds or so. Serve the cooked lamb dish on a serving plate with the pancakes and sauce on the side.

To eat, each diner spoons some of the lamb into the center of a pancake, spreads on the sauce to taste, rolls it up, and eats.

Zen Crisp

○

The original Big Bowl started as a little restaurant with a wildly eclectic selection of dishes, almost all served in a bowl. One of the original menu items was kind of a pizza made with thin Middle Eastern bread, lavash. In changing the menu to all Asian offerings, we kept this idea minus its original toppings, which included cheese. Now we call it a Mongolian Pizza and the version below, which is all-vegetable, has a deliciously rich Northern Chinese eggplant topping layered over a scallion-infused oil that is brushed on the lavash. The eggplant, not entirely necessary, requires its own prepreparation and may be replaced, by cooked chicken for example, or left out entirely.

2 ½ cups thinly sliced scallions

1 teaspoon kosher salt

Peanut or vegetable oil for deep-frying

12 small dried black mushrooms, soaked for 30 minutes in hot water, drained, and thinly sliced

1 medium red pepper

1 pound Asian eggplants (about 3), cut into french fry–sized pieces with skin

½ cup Chinese mushroom soy sauce

½ cup sugar

¼ cup red wine vinegar

2 tablespoons ginger, minced

1 tablespoon garlic, minced

2 pieces lavash flat bread (see Note), cut into thirds

2 tablespoons sesame seeds

Toss the scallions with the salt and let sit for 30 minutes or longer.

Heat ½ cup of the peanut oil over medium heat in a small skillet to hot but not smoking. Remove from the heat and stir in the scallions. They should sizzle slightly but not brown. Remove with the oil immediately to a small bowl and allow to cool.

Heat 3 tablespoons peanut oil in a pan and sauté the mushroom slices and pepper until the pepper is soft. Set aside.

In a wide skillet or wok heat 3 or 4 cups of the peanut oil. Fry the eggplant a few pieces at a time until golden; remove and drain on paper towels.

Combine the soy sauce, sugar, and vinegar, stirring until the sugar dissolves.

Heat a small skillet or saucepan and add 2 teaspoons peanut oil; add the ginger and garlic, and stir briefly. Add the soy sauce–sugar mixture, stirring over high heat just until the sauce boils. Turn off the heat and immediately add the eggplant pieces and toss until they're well coated with the sauce. Set aside.

Preheat the oven to 550 degrees.

Brush the lavash liberally on both sides with more peanut oil. Put the pieces on a sheet pan, place in the oven, and cook both sides until the lavash begins to brown, taking care not to burn, about 1½ minutes. Cool.

(continued)

With a brush, spread the scallion mixture thoroughly on the bread, right to the edge, and sprinkle with the red pepper and mushroom slices. Finally put on the eggplant, trying to keep the skin side up. Finish with a final sprinkling of sesame seeds and place in the preheated oven on a rack. Bake for 1½ minutes. Cut into slices and serve.

NOTE: Lavash is available from Middle Eastern bakeries in sheets of about 12 x 24 inches.

Crispy Flat Bread
with Thai Lamb Curry

○

Flat-bread dishes—that is, thin slices of the Middle Eastern bread lavash, slathered with a topping and baked—are an idea that survived Big Bowl's origins as a hole-in-the-wall with a wildly eclectic menu (see Zen Crisp, page 47). To fit these flat breads in with the current assortment of Asian dishes, we created appropriate toppings such as this lamb suffused with our freshly made curry paste, and we affectionately nicknamed them all "Mongolian pizzas." The topping here, applied in two stages, can be made ahead of time and simply spread on the flat bread and baked to order in a few minutes. This is a great stand-up appetizer for a large group.

FOR THE SCALLION-PEPPER TOPPING

- 2½ cups thinly sliced scallions
- ¼ cup julienned fresh red chile peppers
- 1 teaspoon kosher salt
- ⅔ cup peanut or vegetable oil

To make the scallion-pepper topping, toss the scallion and red pepper with the salt and let sit for 30 minutes or longer.

Heat the peanut oil in a small skillet until it is hot but not smoking. Remove from the heat and stir in the scallions and peppers. They should sizzle slightly but not brown. Remove immediately with the oil to a small bowl, and allow to cool.

FOR THE LAMB CURRY TOPPING

1 pound ground lamb shoulder

1 teaspoon dark soy sauce

2½ tablespoons peanut oil

⅔ cup yellow curry paste (page 16)

1 tablespoon sugar

1 tablespoon freshly squeezed
    lemon juice

4 teaspoons fish sauce

2 pieces lavash (see Note),
    cut into thirds

½ cup chopped roasted peanuts

Cilantro leaves for garnish

To make the lamb curry topping, mix the lamb with the dark soy sauce.

Heat a skillet over medium heat and add the 2½ tablespoons of peanut oil. When hot, add the lamb and sauté just until the lamb changes color and the pieces are broken up, taking care not to brown the meat. Move the lamb off to one side and sauté the curry paste briefly alone; then incorporate it into the lamb by stirring them together. Add the sugar, lemon juice, and fish sauce and turn off the heat. Mix thoroughly and remove to a bowl to cool.

Preheat the oven to 550 degrees.

Brush each of the 6 pieces of lavash liberally on both sides with peanut oil. Put them on a sheet pan and place in the oven and cook on both sides until they begin to brown, taking care not to burn, about 1½ minutes on each side. Cool.

With a brush, spread the scallion-pepper topping thoroughly on the bread, right to the edge. Finally, spread ¼ cup of the lamb curry topping on each piece. Bake for 1½ minutes. Sprinkle each piece with about 1 tablespoon of the chopped peanuts and 8 cilantro leaves. Cut each piece into 5 or 6 triangular slices and serve.

NOTE: Lavash is available from Middle Eastern bakeries in sheets of about 12 x 24 inches.

Serves 10 as an appetizer, 4 to 6 as part of a lunch or supper

Roasted Honey-Lemon Spareribs

○

These tender, glazed ribs, spiced with cinnamon and anise, develop a fine golden brown glaze and, better yet, they can be roasted quickly to finish right before serving.

One 3½-pound rack of spareribs, cut in half across the bone by the butcher

¼ cup kosher salt

1 teaspoon Sichuan peppercorns

3 star anise

One 1-inch stick Chinese cinnamon (cassia)

1 tablespoon plus 2 teaspoons dark soy sauce

3 tablespoons sugar

½ cup honey

½ cup dark corn syrup

3 tablespoons light soy sauce

¼ cup freshly squeezed lemon juice

3 tablespoons julienned fresh red fresno chiles

¼ cup julienned ginger

Zest of 2 lemons, julienned

Rinse and dry the spareribs. Heat a small skillet and toast the salt, Sichuan peppercorns, star anise, and Chinese cinnamon until the spices start to smoke. Remove from the heat. When the spices cool, rub 2 tablespoons of the spice mixture all over the spareribs and allow to sit in an airy place on a rack for at least 4 hours.

Meanwhile, heat 1 tablespoon of the dark soy sauce with the sugar, honey, corn syrup, light soy sauce, lemon juice, chiles, ginger, and lemon zest until the sugar dissolves and the sauce is bubbling. Turn off the heat and transfer to a bowl.

After the ribs have sat, bring about 2 quarts of water to a boil in a large steamer. Put the ribs on a rack above the water, cover and steam them for 45 minutes. Remove from the heat and when cool enough to handle, rub all over with the remaining 2 teaspoons of the dark soy sauce.

Preheat the oven to 500 degrees.

With a brush, slather the ribs generously with the honey-lemon syrup. Put the ribs flat in a baking pan and roast for 6 minutes—the ribs should be inside up. Slide out the ribs, turn them over, and baste liberally with the honey-lemon sauce again. Put back for another 10 minutes. When they develop a golden glaze, remove for the final time and baste again with the honey-lemon sauce.

When the ribs are cool enough, cut them apart and serve with some of the honey-lemon sauce on the side.

Makes about 6 appetizer servings

Not considered a "side dish" in Asia, vegetable dishes have the same status as any other. Fancier vegetable dishes usually have multiple seasonal vegetables, each added during the cooking process at the exact moment when it will be cooked to perfection. The very fanciest have a theme such as "foods of the forest" featuring, for example, various mushrooms, bamboo shoots, black moss, and chestnuts. Here are three markedly unelaborate, simple-to-prepare vegetable dishes we offer at Big Bowl; the Sichuan Green Beans and the Chinese Broccoli with Oyster Sauce are currently on the menu.

Chinese Broccoli with Oyster Sauce

Chinese broccoli, known in Chinese-American markets by its Cantonese name, *gai lan*, is one of the world's most nutritious vegetables, high in calcium, iron, and vitamins A and C. We use it rather than American broccoli in our dishes, mostly because of its flavor. This may be the simplest recipe in the book.

1 pound Chinese broccoli (*gai lan*)
1½ teaspoons oyster sauce
1 teaspoon light soy sauce
½ teaspoon sugar
½ teaspoon sesame oil

Remove and discard the tough ends of the broccoli stems. Cut the rest on the bias into 4-inch lengths, leaves and all. Put in a strainer and add to a pot of rapidly boiling water. Cook until done, 3 to 5 minutes. (It should be bright green and soft with a slight crunch.)

When done, drain thoroughly and arrange on a plate. Mix together oyster sauce, soy sauce, and sugar, and drizzle over the broccoli. Sprinkle over the sesame oil and serve.

Serves 2 to 3 as part of a larger meal

51

Sichuan Green Beans

○

A popular, classic Sichuan Chinese dish, the process here of cooking the beans first in hot oil transforms them into almost a different vegetable—one that is soft, slightly wrinkled, and sweet. Rather than frying, originally these were said to have been cooked until wilted under glass in the hot sun.

1½ pounds fresh string beans (green or yellow wax; or a mixture)

¾ teaspoon salt

1 teaspoon sugar

1 tablespoon Shaoxing rice wine or dry sherry

1 teaspoon white or rice vinegar

1½ cups peanut or vegetable oil

1 cup ground pork (6 ounces)

3 to 6 dried chile peppers, coarsely chopped

2 teaspoons dark soy sauce

Wash the beans, cut off the tips of both ends, dry *thoroughly*, and set aside.

Mix the salt, sugar, wine, and vinegar, and set aside.

Heat the oil in a wok or skillet until very hot. Add the beans in two batches (be careful—the oil is bound to splatter) and cook until wrinkled, 3 minutes or more depending on the freshness of the beans. Remove with a slotted spoon to drain in a colander or on paper toweling and set aside.

Pour off all but 2 tablespoons of the oil. Heat and add the ground pork and dried peppers. Stir over high heat, breaking up the lumps of pork, 2 to 3 minutes. (The pork shouldn't be browned.) Add the soy sauce and stir until evenly colored.

Replace the beans and stir over high heat. Immediately add the salt-sugar-wine mixture and stir over high heat again briefly, about 1 minute. Serve.

Serves 4 as part of a larger meal

Stir-Fried Snow Peas
with Dried Black Mushrooms

○

A fine alternative to snow peas is fresh sugar snap peas, which we buy locally during early summer. This is an easy stir-fry that may be done in a skillet or a wok.

½ pound snow peas (or sugar snap peas)

3 large black dried Chinese mushrooms

3 tablespoons peanut oil

1 heaping teaspoon freshly chopped garlic

¾ teaspoon kosher salt

1½ teaspoons sugar

Few drops sesame oil

String the snow peas.

Cover the mushrooms with boiling water; allow to sit 30 minutes. Remove the mushrooms, reserving 3 tablespoons of the liquid. Cut off and discard the mushroom stems. Cut the caps in half on the bias.

Heat a skillet over high heat and add the peanut oil. When hot, add the mushrooms and stir briefly over high heat. Add the garlic and snow peas, and stir until well coated with the oil. Add the salt, sugar, and reserved mushroom-soaking liquid. Continue to stir over high heat until most of the liquid has disappeared and the peas are crisp yet tender. Serve sprinkled with the sesame oil.

Serves 2 as part of a larger meal

SALADS

On the Eastern Chinese coast, around Shanghai, they've concocted numerous small salads, usually quickly parboiled vegetables tossed in a sesame dressing or freshly made "pickles," with full-flavored and peppery sweet and sour dressings. These small salads are related to similar dishes across the East China Sea in Japan and the various *kimchi* of Korea farther north up the coast.

Both the Hot and Sour Napa Cabbage and the Spicy Daikon and Carrot Pickle that follow are delicious hot fresh pickle condiments to offer diners when they sit down or to serve to complement another dish.

Hot and Sour Napa Cabbage

A fresh spicy, sweet, and very Shanghainese fresh pickle we serve at Big Bowl on special occasions.

1 head napa cabbage (3½ pounds)

1 tablespoon finely julienned fresh ginger

1 tablespoon finely julienned fresh red chile pepper

2 tablespoons plus 1 teaspoon kosher salt

⅓ cup red wine vinegar

⅓ cup Japanese rice wine vinegar

¾ cup sugar

¼ cup peanut oil

5 dried chiles

½ teaspoon Sichuan peppercorns

2 teaspoons sesame oil

Cut the cabbage in half lengthwise and remove the core. Cut across the leaves into a thin julienne. Toss the cabbage with the ginger, fresh red pepper, and 2 tablespoons of salt, and set aside. Let stand for at least 30 minutes.

Meanwhile heat the remaining teaspoon of salt, the vinegars, and the sugar in a saucepan over medium-high heat just until the sugar is dissolved. Remove from the heat.

Heat the peanut oil in a saucepan over medium-high heat with the dried chiles and peppercorns until the peppercorns smoke. Remove from the heat. When the oil cools somewhat, combine it with the vinegar mixture.

After the cabbage has stood, wring out the water by squeezing it in a clean cloth. Put the cabbage into a mixing bowl, combine with 1 cup of the dressing (there may be a little left over), then stir in the sesame oil. Allow to sit for at least 15 minutes, stir, and serve at room temperature.

Makes 10 small servings

Spicy Daikon and Carrot Pickle

○

More like a salad because it should be eaten the day it's made, this fresh pickle is cool, crunchy, sweet, hot, and spicy; it's best eaten as a premeal condiment, as part of a buffet, or as a complement to anything fried. We serve it with Big Bowl Crab Cakes (page 40).

SAUCE

⅓ cup red wine vinegar

⅓ cup Japanese rice wine vinegar

¾ cup sugar

½ teaspoon kosher salt

3 tablespoons peanut oil

5 dried red chile peppers

1 teaspoon Sichuan peppercorns

1 tablespoon finely julienned ginger

1 tablespoon finely julienned
   fresh red chiles

3 pounds daikon (Chinese white
   radish), finely julienned

½ cup finely julienned carrot

2 tablespoons kosher salt

¼ cup thinly sliced scallion

½ cup fresh cilantro leaves

2 teaspoons sesame oil

To make the sauce, combine the vinegars, sugar, and salt in a saucepan and heat over medium-high heat just until the sugar dissolves. Remove the pan from the heat and set aside. Heat a small skillet or saucepan over medium-high heat and add the peanut oil with the dried chiles and Sichuan peppercorns. When the chiles blacken and the peppercorns begin to smoke, turn off the heat and add the ginger and fresh chiles. Immediately stir in the vinegar mixture. Allow to cool.

Meanwhile, mix the daikon and carrot shreds in a bowl with the 2 tablespoons salt, and allow to sit for 1 hour. Putting it a batch at a time in a clean cloth, wring out the moisture from the daikon and carrot, discarding the liquid, and place the vegetables in a mixing bowl.

Mix these shreds with 1 cup of the sauce (there may be a little left over), the scallion, the cilantro leaves, and the sesame oil. Before serving you may want to let the dish sit, mixing the ingredients from time to time.

Serves 8 as an accompaniment to a meal

Spring Asparagus Salad
with Sesame Seeds

○

This colorful and delicious dish, served at room temperature, is typical of the small vegetable salads of China's East Coast. We serve it in the spring at Big Bowl.

1 tablespoon toasted sesame seeds

1½ pounds fresh asparagus

1 tablespoon Japanese rice
    wine vinegar

1 teaspoon red wine vinegar

1 teaspoon fish sauce or
    light soy sauce

1 teaspoon sugar

1 teaspoon Dijon mustard

2 tablespoons fine peanut oil

1 tablespoon sesame oil

In a small skillet, toast the sesame seeds until golden, shaking the pan so they won't burn.

Trim and cut the asparagus into 2-inch lengths. Parboil them in 6 cups water for 2 to 3 minutes, depending on their thickness. Drain and run under cold water to stop the cooking. Dry thoroughly.

Mix together the vinegars, fish sauce, sugar, and mustard. Stir in the oils, combining as you would a vinaigrette. Toss with the asparagus. Sprinkle over the sesame seeds and serve.

Makes 4 to 6 small servings

Fresh Vegetable Early Summer Salad with Light Sesame Dressing

○

Chinese salads rarely use raw vegetables. The vegetables are rather briefly parboiled to bring out a bright color then tossed with a light vinegar and sesame oil dressing.

DRESSING

- 1 teaspoon finely minced garlic
- 1 teaspoon red wine vinegar
- 1 teaspoon fish sauce or light soy sauce
- 1 teaspoon sugar
- 1 teaspoon Dijon mustard
- 2 tablespoons fine peanut oil
- 1 tablespoon sesame oil

- 6 small hearts of Shanghai bok choy, 2½ to 3 inches in length (see Note)
- 10 snow peas
- 1 cup small mixed fresh green and yellow (wax) beans
- ½ cup of chive flowers, stems cut into 2-inch lengths (available in small 10-inch bunches at Chinese markets)
- 1 tablespoon julienned carrot
- 3 fresh water chestnuts, peeled and sliced
- 1 small red fresh chile pepper, julienned

Stir together the garlic, vinegar, fish sauce, sugar, and mustard until the sugar dissolves. Mix in the peanut and sesame oils as you would with any salad dressing.

Bring 6 cups of water to boil and add the bok choy hearts, snow peas, and beans, and cook for 1½ to 2 minutes. For the last 30 seconds, add the carrots, chive flowers, and chive flower stems. When brightly colored and cooked, remove the vegetables to a colander to drain, and rinse under cold water to stop the cooking. Dry well.

When the vegetables are thoroughly dry, combine with the water chestnuts and chile pepper, toss with the dressing, and serve.

NOTE: To get a 2½-inch heart, you simply peel away the leaves of a larger vegetable, reserving them for another use.

Serves 2 to 3 as part of a larger meal

Glazed Sweet-Sour Eggplant
with Sesame Seeds

○

This dish from North China, rich and redolent of ginger and garlic, may be served as a small salad or side dish. It's also wonderful served on toasted croutons (thin slices of baguette brushed with sesame oil and baked on a sheet tray in a 350-degree oven until golden).

1½ pounds Asian eggplants

2 cups or more peanut oil

2 tablespoons dark soy sauce

2 tablespoons sugar

1 tablespoon red wine vinegar

2 tablespoons minced fresh ginger

1 tablespoon minced garlic

½ teaspoon sesame oil

1 tablespoon toasted sesame seeds

Trim the eggplants and slice into french fry-shaped slices about 2 x 2½ inches.

In a deep skillet or wok, heat the oil to 375 degrees. Fry a small batch of eggplant at a time (enough to cover three quarters of the surface of the oil); when golden, remove with a slotted spoon to drain on paper towels. When all batches are fried, remove the oil from the pan (you may strain and save it in a light-proof container for frying or stir-frying).

Mix the soy sauce, sugar, and vinegar.

Heat a clean pan over medium-high heat and add 1 teaspoon of the reserved oil. When hot, add the ginger and garlic, and stir briefly. Add the soy sauce mixture. Cook, stirring, until the mixture blends and thickens slightly (20 seconds or so), and add the reserved eggplant. Turn off the heat and stir the eggplant until well coated with the sauce. Drizzle in the sesame oil.

Serve warm or at room temperature sprinkled with the sesame seeds.

Makes 4 to 6 small servings

Matt McMillin's Vietnamese Caesar Salad

○

For Big Bowl, which prides itself on serving food rooted in tradition, a Southeast Asian Caesar salad seems whacky; but there's a historical linkage that offers some justification—the connection between Italian anchovies and Southeast Asian fish sauce—and the dish works.

We knew, as with modern Thai and Vietnamese cooking, that the main seasoning for the Roman Empire was a fermented fish sauce, called at the time *garum* or *liqueman*; and that the cured anchovy of today is an ancestor of that popular condiment. So we exploited this link between Southeast Asia and ancient Rome in this version of a Caesar by employing a Southeast Asian anchovy sauce called *mam nem* in place of the traditional anchovies.

And we didn't feel bad tampering with it given that, anchovies or not, Caesar salad is not exactly an ancient culinary icon, having been created about 30 years ago in L.A. The dressing below was created by Executive Chef Matt McMillin to be served with Romaine lettuce (and croutons if you wish—see Note), like any Caesar salad.

SAUCE

**2 tablespoons *mam nem*
(a ground fish sauce that comes
in 7-ounce bottles)**

1 tablespoon fish sauce

1 tablespoon Dijon mustard

1 tablespoon red wine vinegar

2 egg yolks

½ tablespoon chopped garlic

⅜ teaspoon kosher salt

1 tablespoon fresh lemon juice

1 teaspoon sugar

½ teaspoon freshly ground black pepper

**1 cup fine peanut oil such as
Lion & Globe (see page 9)**

**5 ounces (about 1 quart) romaine
lettuce, cut into 2 x 2-inch pieces**

Combine all the ingredients, except the oil, in a blender and blend. Add the oil in a steady stream to emulsify. Mix ¼ cup of the dressing (or more to taste) with the romaine.

Serves 2 as the prelude to a meal

NOTE: To make croutons, cut half a loaf of good white bread into ¾-inch cubes, and put in a mixing bowl. Toss with 6 tablespoons of peanut oil, ½ tablespoon kosher salt, 1 tablespoon finely chopped garlic, and ½ teaspoon of freshly ground black pepper. Cook on a sheet pan in a preheated 250-degree oven for 20 to 30 minutes until golden brown and crisp.

Warm Jasmine Rice Salad
with Shrimp and Thai Herbs

○

Matt McMillin, Big Bowl's executive chef, threw together these items for his lunch one day. We ran it as a special the next week. It's simple and delicious.

1 cup just-cooked jasmine rice

2 tablespoons julienned fresh red fresno chile pepper (or other chile)

2 tablespoons ground dried shrimp

2 tablespoons ground golden peanuts (see Note)

⅓ cup finely julienned cucumber

¼ cup fresh cilantro leaves

6 mint leaves, julienned

2 tablespoons fresh lime juice

2 tablespoons fish sauce

1 teaspoon sesame oil

1 tablespoon fine peanut oil

1½ teaspoons sugar

½ teaspoon freshly ground black pepper

6 to 8 medium-large shrimp, butterflied and poached until just done

Mixed greens

When the rice is just cooked and has sat 10 to 20 minutes, combine it with the chile, dried shrimp, peanuts, cucumber, cilantro leaves, and mint.

Combine the lime juice, fish sauce, oils, and sugar, and mix into the rice. Toss in the black pepper and shrimp. Serve on a bed of greens, preferably organic.

NOTE: We recommend starting with raw blanched peanuts (available at Chinese groceries) and browning them in oil (see page 62)

Serves 2

Thai Calamari Salad

○

Midwesterners like squid, although only when it's referred to by its Italian name, calamari. This salad, which we run from time to time as a special, is a jewel of bright traditional Thai flavors. It's as if seasonings such as lime juice, ginger, lemongrass, and Asian basil were designed to go with squid.

12 ounces small squid

½ tablespoon finely julienned ginger

2 tablespoons finely julienned
    fresh red fresno chiles or
    other red chile pepper

1 tablespoon finely julienned scallion
    (green and white)

2 tablespoons julienned cucumber

1 tablespoon thinly sliced red onion

1 tablespoon finely minced lemongrass

1 tablespoon finely julienned celery

6 to 8 Thai basil leaves, julienned

2 tablespoons fresh cilantro leaves

2 tablespoons fish sauce

2 tablespoons fresh lime juice

2 teaspoons sugar

1 teaspoon sesame oil

1 tablespoon fine peanut oil

½ teaspoon freshly ground black pepper

Mesclun (optional)

To clean the squid, cut off the tentacles just below the eyes. Squeeze out the beak and discard it, and put the tentacles into a bowl. Pull out and discard the insides of the squid, including the thin cellophane-like membrane that runs the length of the body. Rinse. Slice the body into ½-inch rings and cut any large tentacles into 2 or 3 sections.

Bring about a quart of water to a boil and add the squid. Cook for 1 minute. Drain and run under cold water to stop the cooking. Dry thoroughly.

Toss the squid with the ginger, chiles, scallion, cucumber, onion, lemongrass, celery, basil, and cilantro. Combine the fish sauce, lime juice, and sugar, stirring until the sugar dissolves. Stir the oils into the fish sauce mixture. Pour the sauce into the salad and mix thoroughly. Sprinkle with the black pepper and mix again.

Serve in individual portions over mesclun greens.

Makes 3 to 4 small servings as the prelude to a meal

Peanut Sauce for Cool Noodles

○

This sauce, which we serve with cold noodles, is native to Sichuan China, and is best made starting from scratch with raw peanuts and served at room temperature.

2 cups fine peanut oil such as Lion & Globe (see page 9)

1 cup blanched peeled raw peanuts (available at Chinese markets)

½ cup freshly brewed Chinese black tea

1 tablespoon chopped ginger

6 garlic cloves

1 to 2 fresh red chile peppers

1 teaspoon kosher salt

1 tablespoon sugar

2 teaspoons dark soy sauce

2 tablespoons light soy sauce

¼ cup Japanese rice wine vinegar

3 tablespoons sesame oil

Chinese egg noodles

Finely julienned seeded and peeled cucumber and fresh cilantro leaves

Heat the peanut oil in a pan to nearly smoking. Add the peanuts, stir once, and turn off the heat. Allow to sit about 10 minutes in the oil until the peanuts are a light golden color. Remove the peanuts with a slotted spoon to a food processor and reserve the oil.

Grind the peanuts to a coarse paste. Add ¼ cup of the reserved oil, a splash of the tea, the ginger, garlic, chile peppers, salt, and sugar and continue to grind. Add the soy sauces and vinegar and grind some more. Remove to a mixing bowl and stir in the oils by hand. Stir in the remaining tea until the sauce is smooth.

Serve over Chinese egg noodles that have been cooked, drained, run under cold water to stop the cooking, drained again, then tossed with 1 teaspoon of sesame oil per ½ pound of cooked noodles. Use ⅔ cup peanut sauce for every pound of cooked noodles and serve with the following garnishes: finely julienned seeded and peeled cucumber and fresh cilantro leaves.

NOTE: Leftover peanut sauce will keep for at least a week in a covered container in the refrigerator.

Makes about 3 cups of sauce

Southeast Asian Pesto

You may have seen this elsewhere, but I've both demonstrated and employed this recipe for a couple of decades and versions of it have since appeared in restaurants and cookbooks. This was originally created as an introduction to Thai flavors for my cooking students in California. At Big Bowl, it's a popular warm-weather special. It's an easy food processor dish.

⅔ cup roasted peanuts (see Note)

1¼ cups fine peanut oil such as Lion & Globe (see page 9)

2 green serrano chiles

1 heaping tablespoon chopped ginger

6 garlic cloves

2 cups Thai basil leaves

⅓ cup mint leaves

⅓ cup coarsely chopped cilantro, leaves and stems

2 teaspoons salt

1½ teaspoons sugar

¼ cup fresh lime juice

Put the peanuts in a food processor with ¼ cup of the oil and grind to a coarse paste. Add the chiles, ginger, and garlic, and continue to grind. Add the herbs, remaining seasonings, and lime juice, adding a little more oil if necessary during the processing.

Transfer to a serving bowl and stir in the remaining oil. Use as a topping for Chinese egg noodles that have been cooked, drained, and lightly oiled. One cup of this sauce should be tossed with 1 pound of cooked noodles.

The dish should be served at room temperature.

Makes about 3 cups of sauce

NOTE: At Big Bowl we start with raw peanuts, which we brown to a light golden in peanut oil (see Peanut Sauce for Cool Noodles, page 62)

Thai Chicken Noodle Salad
with Basil, Lemongrass, and Peanuts

○

A great and unusual summer buffet dish with a pleasing cacophony of Thai flavors. It should be served at room temperature.

1 large whole chicken breast
   (2 halves)

Salt

½ pound fresh Chinese egg noodles
   (regular *mein* from an Asian
   market) or dried spaghetti

2 tablespoons fine peanut oil

1 cucumber, peeled, seeded, and
   julienned

½ small red onion, thinly sliced

3 small fresh red chile peppers,
   seeded and julienned

2 tablespoons finely julienned
   fresh ginger

¼ cup loosely packed Thai (or sweet)
   basil leaves, cut into strips

1 teaspoon finely minced fresh
   lemongrass

2 garlic cloves, minced

¼ cup fresh lime juice

3 tablespoons Thai or Vietnamese
   fish sauce

5 teaspoons sugar

½ teaspoon black pepper

1 teaspoon Sa-te or Chinese chili oil

½ cup fresh cilantro leaves

½ cup chopped roasted or
   fried peanuts

Lightly salt the chicken breast and set aside.

Bring 4 cups water to boil in a saucepan and add the chicken breast (it should be submerged). When the water comes to a boil again, skim, turn off the heat, cover, and let sit about 10 to 15 minutes or until the chicken breast is just cooked. Remove the breast and let cool.

Meanwhile, in a large pot of boiling water, cook the noodles, drain, and run under cold water to stop the cooking. Let drain briefly, toss with 1 tablespoon of the fine peanut oil, and set aside.

When the chicken breast is cool, remove the bone (if any) and skin, and by hand pull the meat apart with the grain into shreds ¼ inch wide and 1½ inches long. Put the meat into a bowl.

Toss the noodles with the cucumber, red onion, chile peppers, ginger, and basil, and set aside.

Combine the lemongrass, garlic, lime juice, fish sauce, sugar, and ½ teaspoon salt, and set aside.

When ready to serve, toss the noodles with the chicken, sauce, remaining tablespoon of peanut oil, herbs, and all the remaining ingredients, except the peanuts. Sprinkle the peanuts over the top and serve.

Serves 2 for lunch, 3 to 4 as part of a larger meal

NOODLE DISHES

MEAL-IN-A-BOWL SOUPS

All-Vegetable Wonton Soup

For people who want an all-vegetable wonton soup with full flavor, we serve this at Big Bowl.

6 dried shiitake mushrooms

EGG CREPES (optional)

2 eggs

1 teaspoon sesame oil

½ cup chopped Sichuan preserved vegetable

2 tablespoons light soy sauce

2 teaspoons sugar

Salt to taste

12 vegetable wontons (see page 28)

6 ounces cooked Shanghai noodles (noodles that have been boiled, run under cold water, drained, and oiled, see page 11)

3 ounces whole spinach leaves (1½ cups)

½ teaspoon sesame oil

Black pepper

Pour 6 cups boiling water over the dried mushrooms and allow to sit for 1 hour. Wring out the mushrooms over the mushroom liquid, reserving the liquid; cut off and discard the mushroom stems, and slice the caps thinly.

The crepes are optional, but they add color and refinement to the soup. To make the crepes, beat the eggs lightly with ½ teaspoon of the sesame oil. Oil a small crepe pan and warm over medium heat. Pour in enough of the egg mixture to coat the bottom, pouring any excess back into the raw egg. When the egg has set, pour it out onto a cutting board. Repeat until all the egg has been used up. Roll the egg crepes and cut into ¼-inch slices. Set aside.

Bring the reserved mushroom liquid to a boil in a saucepan and add the preserved vegetable. Turn the heat to low and simmer the stock, covered, for 30 minutes and add the soy sauce and sugar. Strain the liquid into another pot, heat, and add some salt (it may be fine). Keep it over low heat while you cook the wontons.

Heat 3 quarts water in a large pot. When the water is boiling, add the wontons and cook until they float readily at the surface, about 3 minutes or so. Remove to drain. At the bottom of a large soup bowl, arrange the Shanghai noodles, the egg crepe "noodles," the spinach, and the wontons. Bring the stock to a quick boil, and gently add to the soup bowl.

Sprinkle with the ½ teaspoon sesame oil, add some pepper, and serve.

Serves 2 as a main dish

Hot and Sour Shrimp Soup
with Noodles and Thai Herbs

○

Bursting with all the flavor counterpoints Thai cuisine has to offer—the pungency of chiles, the sourness of lime, the aromatic taste of lemongrass and basil, and the clean, slightly camphorous bite of fresh galangal—this soup undoubtedly has a medicinal as well as a culinary history. It's good and good for you, a low-calorie, meal-in-a-bowl noodle soup that will nourish your body and ward off your cold. It's among the most popular at Big Bowl.

8-ounces dried rice noodles (flat, fettuccine-shaped)

1 pound medium shrimp

Salt

Few drops sesame oil

2 quarts chicken stock, preferably fresh

6 thin slices fresh galangal or fresh ginger

6 garlic cloves, smashed

2 stalks lemongrass (bottom third only, sliced thinly on the bias)

5 shallots, sliced

4 small green serrano chile peppers, coarsely shredded, including seeds

¼ cup Thai or Vietnamese fish sauce

3 teaspoons sugar

¼ cup whole fresh cilantro leaves

¼ cup lightly chopped Asian basil leaves

⅓ cups freshly squeezed lime juice

1 teaspoon freshly ground black pepper

Soak the noodles in hot water to cover and let stand, about 30 minutes, until soft.

Peel the shrimp, reserving the shells. Cut them in half lengthwise, then toss with ¼ teaspoon salt and the sesame oil, and refrigerate.

Bring the stock to a boil with the galangal, garlic, and lemongrass. Turn the heat to low and simmer for 35 minutes. Add the shrimp shells and simmer for another 15 to 20 minutes, skimming if necessary. Strain the stock and bring to a boil. Turn heat to low and simmer with the shallots and chiles. Simmer for 15 minutes and add 2 teaspoons of salt, the fish sauce, and the sugar. Continue to simmer.

Meanwhile, drain the noodles well and divide among four to eight bowls. Then add the shrimp to the simmering broth. Turn off the heat and stir in the fresh herbs and lime juice.

Divide the soup among the soup bowls, sprinkle over the black pepper, and serve.

Makes 4 main dish or 8 small servings

Red Curry Seafood Soup

○

For the chili- and spice-addicted, the heat builds as you eat this soup, which means plucking out and enjoying clams, mussels, scallops, squid—a medly of seafood—between sips of fiery broth.

7-ounces dried rice noodles
    (flat, fettuccine-shaped)

¼ pound daikon (Asian white radish),
    peeled and cut into ½-inch dice

4 cups chicken stock

1 tablespoon peanut oil

½ medium red onion, sliced

4 snow peas, cut into thirds on the bias

4 tablespoons Red Curry Paste
    (page 17)

5 mussels, debearded and scrubbed

6 clams

6 medium shrimp, butterflied

3 sea scallops, cut in half

¼ pound cleaned squid, body cut
    into rings, plus tentacles

¼ teaspoon salt

3½ tablespoons Thai or Vietnamese
    fish sauce

2 teaspoons sugar

¼ cup fresh cilantro leaves

¼ cup Asian basil leaves, julienned

3 tablespoons freshly squeezed
    lemon juice

1 teaspoon freshly ground black pepper

Soak the noodles in hot water to cover and let stand, about 30 minutes, until soft.

Simmer the daikon in ¾ cup chicken stock until soft. Drain, discard the stock, and divide the daikon among four to six soup bowls.

Heat a soup pot over high heat, add the oil, and, when hot, sauté the red onion until translucent; add the snow peas and sauté briefly. Push aside the vegetables and sauté the curry paste to release the flavor. Add the mussels, clams, and ¼ cup of the stock. Simmer just until the mussels and clams open. Take out the shellfish and divide among the soup bowls. Pour the remaining broth into the pot and bring to a boil.

When hot, stir in the shrimp, scallops, and squid. Add ¼ teaspoon of salt, the fish sauce, and the sugar. Turn off the heat under the simmering broth and stir in the fresh herbs and lemon juice. Divide the soup among the soup bowls, sprinkle over the black pepper, and serve.

Serves 4 to 6

Vietnamese Chicken Noodle Soup

○

A longtime offering on our regular menu, this is the most popular soup at Big Bowl. Flavorful and herbaceous, this will also be a sure-fire success for the home cook.

4-ounces dried rice noodles (flat, fettuccine-shaped)

6 ounces boneless chicken breast

1½ teaspoons salt

2 teaspoons cornstarch

1 teaspoon sesame oil

6 cups chicken stock, preferably homemade

3 thin slices fresh ginger

1 garlic clove, smashed

1 stalk lemongrass (bottom third only, sliced thinly on the bias)

2 tablespoons fish sauce

1½ teaspoons sugar

¼ cup Asian basil leaves, lightly chopped

2 tablespoons freshly squeezed lime juice

¼ cup fresh cilantro leaves

1 teaspoon freshly ground black pepper

½ cup fresh bean sprouts

Julienned fresh red or green chile pepper

Lime wedges

Soak the noodles in hot water to cover and let stand, about 30 minutes, until soft.

Cut the chicken breast into julienne-style shreds by first cutting the whole piece horizontally into two large slices. Next stack those slices, cut them into the finest possible shreds, and toss them with ½ teaspoon of the salt, the cornstarch, and the sesame oil. Refrigerate for 30 minutes.

Drop the cold chicken into a small saucepan of boiling water and stir, using chopsticks, to separate the shreds. Just when the meat changes color, drain and run under cold water to stop the cooking; drain again.

Bring the stock to a boil with the ginger, garlic, and lemongrass. Turn the heat to low, simmer, covered, for 35 minutes. Strain the stock, discarding the lemongrass, garlic, and ginger, and heat again. Add 1 teaspoon of salt, the fish sauce, and the sugar. Continue to simmer.

Meanwhile, drain the noodles well and divide among two to four serving bowls. Divide the chicken shreds and basil among the bowls. Add the lime juice to the broth and pour into the soup bowls, sprinkle with the cilantro leaves and black pepper, and serve with the bean sprouts, chiles, and lime wedges on small plates to be added by each diner according to taste.

Serves 2 if it's the main dish, 4 if it's part of a larger meal

Smoked Chicken Noodle Soup
with Napa Cabbage

○

The art of tea-smoking is a specialty of Sichuan, China, where meats such as duck, pork, and chicken are seasoned, steamed, and then smoked over a smoldering combination of black tea, raw rice, sugar, and, sometimes, spices such as star anise and Chinese cinnamon. This soup, a hearty combination of smoked chicken and napa cabbage, is a winter special at Big Bowl.

Leftover roast chicken (or turkey) can be substituted for the chicken here, but not to the same effect.

1 teaspoon peanut oil

4 ounces Tea-Smoked Chicken
  with skin (page 88)

¼ cup sliced bamboo shoots

½ cup sliced napa cabbage

2 tablespoons soaked and
  sliced dry black mushrooms

2½ cups chicken stock

6 ounces noodles, cooked

1 egg crepe, sliced (optional,
  see Note)

2 scallions, sliced

½ teaspoon black pepper

Few drops sesame oil

Heat a skillet, wok, or pot over high heat and add the peanut oil. Add the smoked chicken and cook over high heat for about 30 seconds. Add the bamboo, cabbage, and mushrooms. Cook, stirring, for 2 minutes. Add the chicken stock and bring to a boil. Reduce the heat and simmer for 4 to 5 minutes. Put the noodles in a serving bowl with the egg crepe, if you're using it. Pour over the hot soup and serve garnished with the scallions, black pepper, and sesame oil.

NOTE: To make the egg crepe, beat 1 egg lightly. Heat a small skillet and rub lightly with peanut oil. Pour in the egg, swirl, and when set, remove to a cutting board. Roll and cut into ¼-inch slices.

Serves 3 to 4

Vietnamese Beef Noodle Soup

○

The glory of any soup lies in the broth, a fundamental sometimes overlooked. Created for a surprise birthday supper for friend and colleague Ruth Reichl, here's a composed beef soup that employs a wonderfully full-flavored and complex broth that is beautifully clear and amber. The directions here seem long, but they're not difficult and the rewards are great! The meat and bones are oxtail.

This beef broth is a great base for other, preferably beef, soups. It's delicious served just as a consommé or simply sipped from a mug on a cool day.

4 dried black Chinese mushrooms

4 pounds oxtail, cut into 2-inch lengths by your butcher with base pieces split

½ cup Shaoxing rice wine

2 pieces star anise

One 1-inch lump of yellow rock sugar

1 teaspoon dark soy sauce

1 tablespoon light soy sauce

2 teaspoons kosher salt

½ pound dried Pad Thai rice noodles

½ pound daikon (Asian white radish)

6 to 8 flowering stalks Chinese broccoli (*gai lan*), 4 to 5 inches long

1 tablespoon fish sauce

Freshly ground white pepper

Sesame oil

Cover the mushrooms with ½ cup of hot water and allow to sit for at least 30 minutes.

Rinse the oxtails thoroughly, cover with 8 cups of water, and bring to a boil in a suitable pot. Skim the liquid thoroughly over a period of 10 minutes. Pour in the Shaoxing wine, skim a little more, turn the heat to low, and add the star anise. Simmer, covered, for 30 minutes. Add the sugar, soy sauces, and salt; cover and simmer for another 30 minutes.

Squeeze most of the liquid from the mushrooms, cut off and discard the stems, and, holding the knife on the bias, cut the caps in half. Add the caps to the broth along with the mushroom-soaking liquid. Simmer the caps about 20 minutes, remove with a slotted spoon, and set aside.

Meanwhile pour hot water over the rice noodles and allow to soak for around 30 minutes. When softened, remove, rinse with cold water, and drain.

Peel and cut the radish into 2-inch-long french fry–shaped pieces. Simmer in the soup broth until translucent and soft, about 30 minutes. Remove with a slotted spoon and set aside. In a separate pot of boiling water, blanch the broccoli stalks for about 1 minute, then rinse under cold water, and set aside.

(continued)

At the end of 90 minutes to 2 hours, check the oxtail. If the meat is soft and beginning to fall off of the bone, remove about one third of the pieces. Turn off the heat under the stockpot, scoop off 1 cup of the broth, pour it into a small pot, and allow the rest to sit, covered, for 30 minutes.

Bring the cup of stock to a boil to reduce it while you separate the meat from the bone of the oxtail you removed. When the stock has reduced to nearly a glaze, about ¼ cup, toss with the oxtail meat and set aside.

Strain the beef broth from the stockpot with a fine strainer into a clean pot, add the fish sauce, and heat to boiling.

Divide the rice noodles (you may not need them all) among 4 to 6 preferably flat soup bowls. Then, with some care, arrange the oxtail meat, mushroom slices, radish, and Chinese broccoli among the bowls. When the stock comes to a boil, turn off the heat, and carefully ladle the broth into the bowls. Sprinkle each bowl with white pepper and a few drops of sesame oil and serve.

Serves 4 to 6

7 CHINESE EGG NOODLES

Kung Pao Chickenless Egg Noodles

○

The name of this dish, plucked from our menu, is meant to imply (humorously) a vegetarian version of Kung Pao chicken, combined with noodles. It's a fiery, very garlicky, gutsy dish with authentic Sichuan flavor that satisfies meat eaters and non-meat eaters alike.

8 ounces fresh Chinese egg noodles

Peanut oil for deep-frying plus 1 teaspoon

1 cup diced bean curd (cut into ¾-inch dice)

1½ cups raw peanuts, lightly chopped (see Note)

2 teaspoons chili paste with garlic

1½ tablespoons bean sauce

1 tablespoon hoisin sauce

1 tablespoon Chinese light soy sauce

1 tablespoon sugar

1 tablespoon red wine vinegar

6 to 8 dried whole chiles, coarsely crushed if you want this really hot

½ cup sliced scallions (white only, ½-inch slices)

8 whole garlic cloves, smashed

2 tablespoons Shaoxing rice wine or dry sherry

2 cups cilantro leaves

Bring a large quantity of water to boiling and cook the egg noodles as you would any pasta, around 5 minutes or until done. Drain, run under cold water to stop the cooking, drain again, and toss with 1 teaspoon of the peanut oil. Set aside.

Heat 2 to 3 cups of oil in a wok or skillet until hot but not smoking, and add the bean curd. Turn gently in the oil and fry until golden. Remove the bean curd with a slotted spoon to drain on paper towels.

Add the peanuts to the same oil and stir gently for 10 seconds; turn off the heat and allow to sit until the peanuts are a light golden. Remove them with a slotted spoon to drain on paper towels. When cool, remove and gently chop ¼ cup; set aside. Reserve the oil.

Mix together the chili paste, bean sauce, hoisin sauce, soy sauce, sugar, and vinegar, and keep handy.

(continued)

BIG BOWL

73

In a clean wok or skillet, heat 4 tablespoons of the reserved oil. As it's heating, add the chile peppers and cook over medium heat until they blacken and smoke. Quickly turn the heat to high, add scallion whites, and cook, stirring, 5 seconds; add the garlic and the sauce mixture and cook until bubbling hot.

Add the noodles and cook until well coated with the sauce. Add the fried bean curd and stir. Splash in the Shaoxing; add most of the ¾ cup whole peanuts, turn off heat, and stir in the cilantro. Sprinkle the reserved chopped peanuts on top and serve.

NOTE: You may use already-roasted peanuts for this dish.

Serves 2 as a meal or 3 to 4 as part of a larger meal

Hot and Sour Shrimp Spaghetti

○

*V*inegary and hot, slightly sweet, these noodles are loaded with flavor.

2 large dried black mushrooms

6 ounces fresh Chinese egg noodles
    or 6 ounces dried spaghetti

¾ cup or so peanut oil

8 fresh shrimp, deveined and
    cut in half lengthwise

2 teaspoons cornstarch

1 teaspoon sesame oil plus a few drops

2 tablespoons red wine vinegar

2 tablespoons rice vinegar

7 teaspoons light soy sauce

2 tablespoons sugar

8 dried chiles

4 freshly peeled fresh water chestnuts,
    sliced

2 tablespoons finely chopped fresh ginger

1 tablespoon finely chopped fresh garlic

½ cup finely sliced scallion (white only)

½ cup finely sliced scallion (green)

Soak the dried mushrooms in hot water to cover for 30 to 60 minutes. Discard soaking water. Squeeze out the moisture, cut off and discard the stems, and slice thinly.

Bring a large quantity of water to boiling and cook the egg noodles as you would any pasta, around 5 minutes or until done. Drain, run under cold water to stop the cooking, drain again, and toss with 1 teaspoon of the peanut oil. Set aside.

Toss the shrimp with the cornstarch and 1 teaspoon of the sesame oil.

Combine the vinegars, soy sauce, and sugar; set aside.

Heat the peanut oil in a wok or skillet until hot but not smoking. Add the shrimp and cook, stirring just to separate. When the shrimp changes color, remove to drain in a colander. Reserve the oil.

Heat a clean wok or skillet and add 5 tablespoons of the reserved oil and the dried chiles. Cook over medium-high heat until the chiles blacken and smoke. Add the mushroom slices and stir briefly. Add the water chestnuts, ginger, garlic, and scallion whites, and stir briefly and rapidly, taking care not to brown the garlic. Turn the heat to high and add the vinegar mixture. Bring quickly to a boil. Add the noodles and the shrimp and toss until hot. Toss in the green scallions and serve sprinkled with a few drops of sesame oil.

Serves 1 hungry person, 2–3 as part of a larger meal

Egg Noodles with Calamari, Ginger, and Chinese Black Beans

○

People even remotely adventurous will love this dish. It has a wonderful earthy taste with its fermented black beans, garlic, and ginger; and the fresh chile shreds give it some bite. It's also great-looking.

½ pound fresh squid, cleaned

8 ounces fresh Chinese egg noodles (regular *mein* from an Asian market)

¼ cup peanut or vegetable oil

⅓ cup chicken stock

½ teaspoon kosher salt

1½ teaspoons sugar

2 tablespoons oyster sauce

1 tablespoon light soy sauce

¼ cup finely shredded fresh ginger

1 cup sliced scallions

2 tablespoons shredded fresh red chile pepper

1 tablespoon minced garlic

1½ teaspoons salted Chinese black beans

2 tablespoons Shaoxing rice wine or dry sherry

½ teaspoon sesame oil

Cut the squid bodies into ½-inch-wide rings and cut the tentacles in half if large or, if you want to be a little fancier, do the following: split the whole body of the squid with a knife and lay it inside up on a cutting board. Holding the knife nearly parallel to the squid, score the body with straight cuts, ¼ inch apart, taking care not to cut through. Turn the body 90 degrees and repeat so you have a crosshatch pattern. Cut the body into six more or less equal pieces and add to a bowl with the tentacles. Repeat with all the squid.

Bring a pot of water to a boil, add the squid, and cook, stirring to separate the pieces, about 20 seconds. Drain and rinse under cold water to stop the cooking. Set on paper towels to dry.

Bring a large amount of water to boiling and cook the Chinese noodles as you would any pasta, around 5 minutes or until done. Drain, run under cold water to stop the cooking, drain again, and toss with 1 teaspoon of the peanut oil. Set aside.

Mix the chicken stock with the salt, sugar, oyster sauce, and light soy sauce and keep handy.

Heat a wok or heavy skillet over high heat. When very hot, add the remaining oil. When hot, add the ginger, scallions, chile pepper shreds, garlic, and black beans. Cook stirring for 30 seconds until fragrant.

Add the seasoned chicken stock mixture and cook until the sauce boils. Add the cooked noodles and toss the noodles over high heat for 1 to 2 minutes, or until heated thoroughly. Add the squid and the wine, and toss until piping hot. Drizzle over the sesame oil and serve.

Serves 3 to 4

Thai Red Curry Noodles with Clams

Classy and delicious, this is best with small manila clams from the West Coast or littlenecks from the East Coast.

6 ounces Chinese egg noodles or 6 ounces dried noodles

2 tablespoons plus 1 teaspoon peanut oil

12 to 14 clams, scrubbed

1 tablespoon fish sauce

1 tablespoon fresh lime juice

1 ½ teaspoons sugar

2 tablespoons julienned fresh sweet or hot red peppers

12 snap peas

3 tablespoons Red Curry Paste (page 17)

¼ cup chicken stock

2 tablespoons chopped roasted peanuts

Bring a large amount of water to boiling and cook the Chinese noodles as you would any pasta, around 5 minutes or until done. Drain, run under cold water to stop the cooking, drain again, and toss with 1 teaspoon of the peanut oil. Set aside.

Put the clams in a saucepan, add ¼ cup of water, cover, and steam open over high heat. When just opened, turn off the heat and remove the clams with a slotted spoon to a bowl, and set aside. Pour 2 tablespoons of the remaining liquid into a mixing bowl and discard the rest.

Add the fish sauce, fresh lime juice, and sugar to the clam liquid in the mixing bowl.

Heat a wok or skillet and add the remaining 2 tablespoons oil. When hot, add the peppers and snap peas, and stir until well coated with the hot oil. Pushing the vegetables aside, add the curry paste and stir briefly to release the flavor.

Add the chicken stock and bring to a rapid boil. Add the noodles and toss until hot, 1 to 2 minutes. Add the clams and toss gently to mix. Add the fish sauce–clam juice mixture and toss until the noodles are piping hot. Pour unto a serving plate, sprinkle with the peanuts, and serve.

Serves 2 to 3 as part of a larger meal

Chicken with Spring Asparagus and Chinese Egg Noodles

○

This is dish appears with the first asparagus and runs through their season. Asparagus complements the winy, rustic taste of Chinese salted and fermented black beans.

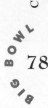

8 ounces fresh Chinese egg noodles (regular *mein* from Asian market)

Peanut or vegetable oil

6 ounces boneless chicken breast, thinly sliced

3 teaspoons cornstarch

1 teaspoon salt

2½ teaspoons sesame oil

¼ pound asparagus

½ cup chicken stock

2 tablespoons oyster sauce

1 tablespoon light soy sauce

1½ teaspoons sugar

½ cup sliced fresh mushrooms (may include oyster mushrooms or fresh shiitakes)

2 teaspoons minced ginger

2 teaspoons minced garlic

1 tablespoon shredded fresh red chile pepper

1½ teaspoons salted Chinese black beans

2 tablespoons Shaoxing rice wine or dry sherry

Bring a large amount of water to boiling and cook the Chinese noodles as you would any pasta, around 5 minutes or until done. Drain, run under cold water to stop the cooking, drain again, and toss with 1 teaspoon of the peanut oil. Set aside.

Combine the chicken with 1½ teaspoons cornstarch, ½ teaspoon salt, and 2 teaspoons of the sesame oil, and set aside or refrigerate.

Peel the asparagus, if necessary, and cut them on the bias into 2-inch lengths.

Mix the chicken stock with the remaining ½ teaspoon salt, the oyster sauce, light soy sauce, and sugar; keep handy.

Mix the remaining 1½ teaspoons cornstarch with 2 tablespoons water.

Heat 1 cup of the peanut or vegetable oil in a wok or heavy skillet to hot but not smoking. Add the chicken and stir just until it changes color. Remove and drain, reserving the oil.

Heat a wok or heavy skillet over high heat. When hot, add 3 tablespoons of the reserved oil. When oil is hot, add the mushrooms. Cook over medium heat for 1 to 2 minutes or until cooked. Add the ginger, garlic, shredded chiles, and black beans, and cook briefly, until fragrant.

Add the asparagus and toss until coated with the oil and seasonings. Add the seasoned chicken stock mixture and cook, stirring, until the sauce boils. Lower the heat and simmer until the asparagus is just cooked. Re-add the chicken, stir, then add the cooked noodles. Turn the heat to high and toss the noodles for 1 to 2 minutes, or until heated thoroughly. The sauce should be reduced.

Recombine the cornstarch and water and add. Continue to cook until the noodles are thoroughly hot and have a clear sheen. Add the Shaoxing or sherry. Toss briefly. Serve garnished with the remaining ½ teaspoon sesame oil.

Serves 2 if it's the whole meal, 3 to 4 as part of a larger meal

Thai Chicken Noodles
with Garlic and Peanuts

○

The essence of Thai flavor is in this simple noodle dish. It's almost like a fragrant, flavorful warm noodle salad. In fact this can be cooled to room temperature and served as such.

6 ounces fresh or dried Chinese egg noodles

Peanut or vegetable oil

3 tablespoons fish sauce

2½ tablespoons fresh lime juice

1 tablespoon sugar

6 ounces boneless chicken breast, julienned

¼ teaspoon kosher salt

2 teaspoons cornstarch

1 teaspoon sesame oil

2 tablespoons julienned, seeded fresh red chiles or bell peppers

¼ cup thinly sliced red onion

¼ cup 1-inch scallion segments

2 tablespoons julienned ginger

6 garlic cloves, smashed

12 Thai basil leaves, julienned

¼ cup fresh cilantro leaves

⅓ cup roasted peanuts, lightly chopped

Bring a large amount of water to boiling and cook the Chinese noodles as you would any pasta, around 5 minutes or until done. Drain, run under cold water to stop the cooking, drain again, and toss with 1 teaspoon of the peanut oil. Set aside.

Mix the fish sauce, lime juice, and sugar, and set aside.

Mix the chicken with the salt, cornstarch, and sesame oil, and refrigerate until ready to cook.

In a wok or skillet, heat 1 cup peanut oil. When hot but not smoking, add the chicken shreds and cook, stirring to separate the shreds. Just when the chicken changes color, remove and drain in a colander. Reserve the oil.

Heat a clean wok or skillet. When very hot, add 4 tablespoons of the reserved oil. When hot, add the chiles, onion, and scallion and stir briefly over high heat to coat with the oil. Add the ginger and garlic, and continue to stir. Add the fish sauce mixture and, when it starts to a boil, add the noodles and toss until well heated. Stir in the basil and cilantro, and toss. Sprinkle in half the peanuts and immediately transfer to a serving plate. Sprinkle the rest of the peanuts on top.

Serves 2 to 3 as part of a larger meal

Sichuan Garlic Noodles
with Blackened Chiles and Peanuts

The sauce here, slightly sweet and redolent of garlic, chiles, and wine, has a taste that is compelling and exotic. It's an authentic Sichuan Chinese flavor featuring bean sauce, a taste that also permeates the cooking of Taiwan. A little west of that, we've found the dish is hungrily received by Midwestern Americans and is a mainstay of our regular menu.

8 ounces fresh Chinese egg noodles

Peanut or vegetable oil

5 ounces boneless chicken breast, thinly sliced

1 teaspoon cornstarch

¼ teaspoon salt

½ teaspoon sesame oil

2 tablespoons whole bean sauce

1 tablespoon hoisin sauce

2 teaspoons chili paste with garlic

1 tablespoon red wine vinegar

1 tablespoon sugar

4 to 6 dried hot red chiles

1 teaspoon chopped fresh ginger

1 tablespoon fresh chopped garlic

½ cup sliced scallions (whites)

¼ cup chicken broth

⅓ cup whole unsalted peanuts, oven-roasted and lightly chopped

1 cup cilantro leaves

1 tablespoon sliced scallion greens

Few drops sesame oil

Bring a large amount of water to boiling and cook the Chinese noodles as you would any pasta, around 5 minutes or until done. Drain, run under cold water to stop the cooking, drain again, and toss with 1 teaspoon of the peanut oil. Set aside.

Mix the chicken slices with cornstarch, salt, and sesame oil, and set aside.

Mix the bean sauce, hoisin, chili paste, vinegar, and the sugar, and set aside.

Heat a wok or skillet and add 1 cup oil. When hot but not smoking, add the chicken and cook until the meat changes color. Remove with a slotted spoon to drain. Remove and reserve the oil.

Heat a clean skillet or wok over high heat. When hot, add 4 tablespoons of the reserved oil and add the dried chiles. Cook until they blacken and smoke. Add the ginger, garlic, and scallion whites, and stir very briefly. Add the sauce mixture and cook, stirring, until it boils.

Add the noodles and the reserved chicken and toss until well coated. Add the chicken broth and toss until most of the liquid disappears. Turn off the heat, stir in the peanuts, cilantro, and scallion greens, and serve sprinkled with the sesame oil.

Serves 2 as the mainstay of a meal, 3 to 4 as part of a larger meal

Hunan Spaghetti

○

Named with Marco Polo in mind, this dish features chicken plus a ground pork sauce loaded with ginger, garlic, chili paste, and bean sauce—the lusty flavors of Hunan Province in Southwestern China.

8 ounces fresh Chinese egg noodles

Peanut or vegetable oil

¼ pound boneless chicken breast, cut into ½-inch cubes

3 teaspoons cornstarch

¼ teaspoon salt

1½ teaspoons sesame oil

2 tablespoons bean sauce

1 tablespoon chili paste with garlic

2 teaspoons sugar

1 tablespoon Shaoxing rice wine

1½ tablespoons chopped ginger

1½ tablespoons chopped garlic

¼ cup scallion whites

1 tablespoon chopped fresno chiles

⅓ pound ground pork, preferably not lean

1 teaspoon dark soy sauce

⅔ cup chicken stock

1 teaspoon cornstarch mixed with 1 tablespoon water

½ cup sliced scallion greens

Bring a large amount of water to boiling and cook the noodles as you would any pasta, around 5 minutes or until done (beyond al dente). Drain, run under cold water, drain again, and toss with 1 teaspoon of the peanut oil. Set aside.

Combine the chicken breast with 1 teaspoon cornstarch, ¼ teaspoon salt, and 1 teaspoon sesame oil, and set aside or refrigerate.

Mix the bean sauce, chili paste with garlic, sugar, and wine; set aside.

Mix the remaining 2 teaspoons of cornstarch with 2 tablespoons water.

Heat 1 cup oil in a wok or heavy skillet to hot but not smoking. Add the chicken and cook, stirring, just until the chicken changes color. Remove and drain, reserving the oil.

Heat a clean wok or large skillet over high heat. When hot, add 2 tablespoons of the reserved oil. When hot, add the ginger, garlic, scallions, and fresno chiles, and stir briefly until fragrant. Add the pork and stir, pressing the meat until the grains separate and turn color. Do not brown. Add the dark soy sauce and cook, stirring, until the meat is evenly colored.

Add the bean sauce–chili paste mixture and cook, stirring, until thoroughly mixed. Pour in the chicken stock and cook until bubblingly hot, about 2 to 3 minutes. Add the noodles and cook, tossing with the sauce. Add the chicken and stir in to reheat.

Give the cornstarch mixture a stir to recombine thoroughly and add. Cook, stirring over high heat, until the dish appears glazed. Stir in the scallion greens and remove to a serving plate. Sprinkle with the remaining sesame oil and serve.

Serves 2 as a meal, 3 to 4 as part of a larger meal

Thai Yellow Curry Beef Noodles

○

The best possible curry noodles, the lineage of this recipe goes back one decade through three restaurants to Monsoon in San Francisco, where they were offered with fresh manila clams or large Gulf shrimp.

½ pound fresh Chinese egg noodles

Peanut or vegetable oil

6 ounces flank steak

½ tablespoon dark soy sauce

1 teaspoon sesame oil

1 teaspoon cornstarch

⅓ cup chicken stock

1 teaspoon kosher salt

4 teaspoons fish sauce

1 tablespoon fresh lime juice

1½ teaspoons sugar

2 tablespoons julienned fresh red chile peppers (we use fresnos)

¼ cup thinly sliced red onion

12 to 15 snow or snap peas

2 heaping tablespoons Yellow Curry Paste (page 16)

¼ cup cilantro leaves

½ cup coarsely ground peanuts, roasted

Bring a large amount of water to boiling and cook the noodles as you would any pasta, around 5 minutes or until done (beyond al dente). Drain, run under cold water to stop the cooking, drain again, and toss with 1 teaspoon of the peanut oil. Set aside.

Slice the flank steak as thinly as possible across the grain into 2-inch lengths. Mix with the soy sauce, sesame oil, and cornstarch, and set aside.

Mix the chicken stock with the salt and fish sauce. Mix the lime juice and sugar; set both mixtures conveniently aside.

Heat 1 cup oil in a wok or small skillet to hot but not smoking. Add the beef and stir just to separate the slices. Remove and drain when still pink in the center. Reserve the oil.

Heat a clean wok or skillet. When hot, add 2 tablespoons of the reserved oil. When the oil is hot, add the chiles, onion, and snow peas, and cook, tossing rapidly until well coated with the oil. Shove the vegetables to the side and add the curry paste. Stir the paste around briefly to release its flavor, and add the seasoned stock. Bring to a full-fledged boil, then add the noodles.

Cook, stirring or tossing (if it's in your repertoire) the noodles until mixed with the sauce and vegetables. Add the beef and toss briefly. Add the lime juice–sugar mixture and toss until the whole mixture is hot. Remove from the heat, stir in the cilantro, remove to a plate, sprinkle with the peanuts, and serve.

Serves 2 as a complete meal, 4 as part of a larger meal

Blazing Big Rice Noodles with Beef (page 102)

○ Thai Red Curry Noodles with Clams (page 77)
and Stir-Fried Snow Peas with Dried Black Mushrooms (page 53)

Pad Thai with Wok-Seared Salmon (page 96)

○ Shrimp with Fresh-Shucked Corn
and Sugar Snap Peas (page 134)

Braised Baby Spareribs
with Black Beans and Garlic
(clay pot, page 143)
and Roasted Honey-
Lemon Spareribs (page 50)

Indonesian Chicken and Beef
Satays with Peanut Sauce
(page 21) and Spicy Daikon
and Carrot Pickle (page 55)

Spring Asparagus with Chicken Stir-Fry
(page 110)

○ Green Vegetable "Steamer Basket"
Wontons with Chinese Chives and
Mustard Greens (page 28)

Salmon Dumplings with Coconut Curry Sauce
(page 30)

 Thai Chicken Soong
(page 24)

Loin of Lamb
Mu Shu Wrap
(page 46)

O Pan-Roasted
Shrimp-Stuffed
Chile Peppers
(page 36)

O Sea Scallops with
Tomatoes and Fresh
Water Chestnuts
(page 137)

Spring Asparagus Salad with Sesame Seeds (page 56) and Alaskan Halibut with Cantonese Lemon–Black Bean Sauce (page 126)

○ Steamed Mussels
in Coconut Herb
Broth (page 34)

○ Egg Noodles with
Calamari, Ginger,
and Chinese Black Beans
(page 76)

Thai Chicken Noodles with Garlic and Peanuts (page 79)

Stir-Fried Hunan Pork Loin
with Fresh Chiles and
Bamboo Shoots (page 141)

Shanghai Noodles with Smoked Chicken (page 90)

Lamb with Basil Noodles

○

Lots of fresh Thai basil, tender shreds of lamb, and a light coconut cream sauce spiked with a squeeze of fresh lime makes this an exceptional noodle dish. Chinese egg noodles of this sort, by the way, are a staple in Thailand, where they're called *ba mee.*

6 ounces fresh Chinese egg noodle

Peanut oil

⅔ cup coconut milk

1 tablespoon minced ginger

2 tablespoons fish sauce

6 ounces lamb shoulder

1 teaspoon dark soy sauce

1 teaspoon sesame oil

½ cup finely sliced red onion

¼ cup julienned fresh red chile pepper

¼ cup chicken stock

½ teaspoon salt

⅓ cup tightly packed Thai basil leaves

Juice of ½ large lime

½ teaspoon freshly ground black pepper

Cilantro for garnish

Cook noodles in a large quantity of boiling water, like any pasta. Drain, run under cold water; drain again. Toss with 1 teaspoon of the peanut oil and set aside.

Simmer the coconut milk in a stainless steel pan for 5 minutes. Add the ginger and continue simmering until the milk reduces to ½ cup. Stir in the fish sauce and turn off the heat.

Marinate the lamb in the dark soy sauce and sesame oil; set aside for at least 15 minutes.

Heat 1 cup peanut oil in a pot or wok until hot but not smoking. Turn off the heat, add the lamb, and cook, separating the slices, until the meat starts to change color but remains rare. Remove and drain in a small colander; reserve the oil.

Heat a clean wok or skillet over high heat, add 2 tablespoons of the reserved oil, and, when hot, add the red onion and chiles and stir until the onion turns translucent. Add the reserved coconut milk and the chicken stock, sprinkle in the salt, and bring to a simmer. Add the noodles and lamb and toss until hot. Add the basil and toss briefly. Add the fresh lime juice. Toss and serve sprinkled with the pepper and garnished with cilantro.

Serves 2 as main dish, 3 to 4 as part of a larger meal

Two Sides Golden Noodle Cake
(Chow Mein)

○

A classic home-style feast of a dish where a mound of egg noodles is pan-fried to a golden brown on two sides. Crispy on the outside and still soft in the middle, this cake is then smothered with multiple ingredients—shrimp, beef, chicken, mushrooms, bok choy, all in a light chicken stock sauce—and served as a meal unto itself. The version below is topped with a bright yellow egg crepe cut like fettuccine.

For those who recall the earliest Chinese-American *chow mein*, it was this dish that became abbreviated to its main component (shrimp, beef, chicken) embedded in a gooey celery and onion topping, and spread over little fried noodles that came in a can. Please enjoy the original.

Cover the black mushrooms with ½ cup boiling water and let soak for at least 30 minutes.

Bring a large quantity of water to boiling and cook the noodles as you would any pasta, about 5 minutes. Drain the noodles, run under cold water to stop the cooking, and drain well again. Toss with 1 teaspoon of sesame oil and set aside.

To make the egg crepes, beat the 2 eggs lightly with ¼ teaspoon sesame oil. Heat a small pan or skillet over medium heat and add a few drops of oil just to coat the bottom. When hot add a ladleful of the egg and swirl around the hot pan until it covers the bottom. Pour any excess back into the bowl. Cook briefly over medium heat, just until the eggs set, and turn out onto a cutting board (the egg should not brown). Wipe the pan with an oil-dampened paper towel and repeat the process until the eggs are gone. Stack the egg crepes, roll up, and cut into ¼-inch widths. The egg crepes will now have the shape of flat noodles.

In three individual small individual bowls toss the shrimp, chicken, and flank steak each with 1 teaspoon of sesame oil and 1 teaspoon cornstarch. Mix the dark soy sauce into the flank steak.

Mix together the chicken broth, oyster sauce, light soy sauce, salt, and sugar; set aside. Mix ¼ cup of the soaking liquid with the remaining 5 teaspoons of cornstarch.

Remove the black mushrooms from the water, squeeze out the liquid, and thinly slice; set aside.

4 dried black mushrooms

8 ounces fresh Chinese egg noodles

4 teaspoons sesame oil

EGG CREPES

2 eggs

¼ teaspoon sesame oil plus a few
    drops for coating pan

3 ounces peeled shrimp, cut in half
    lengthwise

3 ounces boneless chicken breast,
    sliced

3 ounces flank steak, thinly sliced
    across the grain

1 teaspoon dark soy sauce

8 teaspoons cornstarch

1¾ cups chicken broth

2 tablespoons oyster sauce

1 tablespoon light soy sauce

2 teaspoons salt

2 teaspoons sugar

2 cups peanut oil

¼ pound fresh mushrooms, sliced

1 tablespoon julienned carrots

2 tablespoons julienned bamboo
    shoots

1 tablespoon julienned ginger

2 teaspoons chopped garlic

8 ounces hearts of bok choy,
    cut in half

2 ounces snow peas

1 to 2 fresh red chile peppers, seeded
    and julienned

1½ tablespoons cornstarch mixed
    with 4½ tablespoons water

½ teaspoon black pepper

Over high heat bring a round-bottom pan or wok to hot and add ½ cup peanut oil. When hot add the noodles and adjust them with a spoon so that they form an 8-inch nest. Over medium-high heat let the noodles cook about 10 minutes, until they brown lightly. With a spatula and slotted spoon, turn the noodles to the other side. They should brown on that side in 3 to 5 minutes. Remove to a large serving platter with a slotted spoon. (The noodle cake should be light brown and crispy on the outside while maintaining its soft noodle texture within.)

Add the remaining 1½ cups peanut oil to the pan and heat to hot but not smoking. One at a time add the shrimp, chicken, and beef to the oil. Stir briefly to separate the pieces and remove each and drain in the same colander just as it changes color. Remove the oil from the pan and reserve.

Heat a clean wok or large skillet over high heat and add 4 tablespoons of the reserved oil. When hot add the fresh mushrooms and sauté until they begin to soften. Add the black mushroom slices and continue stirring. Add the carrots, bamboo, ginger, and garlic, and stir briefly. Add the bok choy, snow peas, and chile peppers and cook, tossing until well coated with the oil. Add the chicken broth mixture and bring to a boil.

Re-add the shrimp, chicken, and beef, and cook briefly just to heat. Restir the cornstarch-mushroom liquid mixture and cook until the sauce thickens slightly and becomes clear. Pour over the noodle cake. Sprinkle over 1 teaspoon of sesame oil and the pepper. Garnish with the egg crepe and serve by making sure each person gets a little of the noodle cake with his seafood, meat, and vegetables.

Serves 3 to 4 as a complete meal

SHANGHAI NOODLES

Shanghai Noodles with Vegetables and Eggplant

○

This is a wonderful vegetable dish in which any combinations of vegetables could be married with these exquisite noodles. The topping of golden eggplant "fries" gives the dish a great look and taste.

2 large black dried mushrooms

½ pound fresh Shanghai noodles

1½ teaspoons sesame oil

2½ tablespoons oyster sauce

1 tablespoon light soy sauce

1½ teaspoons sugar

¼ teaspoon kosher salt

¼ cup chicken stock

1 cup plus 3 tablespoons peanut or vegetable oil

¾ cup Asian eggplant, cut into french fry–size pieces (skin included)

1 teaspoon minced garlic

1 tablespoon julienned carrot

2 tablespoons julienned bamboo shoots

¼ cup scallions cut into 2-inch lengths

4 ounces small bok choy hearts, cut into quarters, or bok choy leaves and stems cut into 2-inch lengths

12 snow or snap peas

½ cup bean sprouts

½ teaspoon freshly ground black pepper

Put the dried mushrooms in a bowl, cover with hot tap water, and soak for 30 minutes or longer.

Bring a large quantity of unsalted water to boil and cook the noodles as you would any pasta, about 5 minutes. Drain, run under cold water, drain again, and toss with a teaspoon of sesame oil. Set aside.

Mix the oyster sauce, light soy sauce, sugar, and salt with the chicken stock and set aside. Wring out the mushrooms, remove and discard the stems, and slice.

Heat 1 cup peanut oil in a wok or small skillet to hot but not smoking. Fry the eggplant a few pieces at a time until golden brown. Drain on paper towels.

Heat a clean wok or skillet over high heat and add 3 tablespoons oil. When hot, add the garlic, toss briefly, and add the carrot, mushrooms, bamboo, and scallions, and cook over high heat, tossing rapidly for about 30 seconds. Add the bok choy and snow peas, and continue to toss for another minute. Add the seasoned stock and bring to a boil while turning the vegetables. Add the noodles and cook, stirring, until the noodles are piping hot and most of the sauce is reduced away.

Add the bean sprouts, remove from the heat, and toss. Pour onto a serving platter and sprinkle with the eggplant. Drizzle over the remaining ½ teaspoon sesame oil and serve.

Serves 2 as a meal, and 4 as part of a larger meal

Shanghai Noodles
with Shrimp and Fresh Vegetables

Known as "Shanghai with Shrimp" at Big Bowl, this is a simple shrimp with vegetables noodle dish reminiscent of the original Chinese-American *lo mein*—except that authentic, hand-cut Shanghai noodles are relatively new to these shores.

8 ounces Shanghai noodles

3 teaspoons sesame oil plus few
　　drops for sprinkling

3 large dried black mushrooms

6 ounces large fresh shrimp

1 teaspoon cornstarch

4 ounces small bok choy leaves
　　with stems

¼ cup bamboo shoots, sliced

3 scallions, cut into 2-inch lengths

¼ cup unseasoned chicken stock

3 tablespoons oyster sauce

1 tablespoon light soy sauce

1½ teaspoons sugar

½ teaspoon salt

½ cup peanut or vegetable oil

½ cup bean sprouts

Freshly ground black pepper

Cook the noodles in a large quantity of rapidly boiling water, drain, run under cold water to stop the cooking, and drain again. Toss with 2 teaspoons of the sesame oil and set aside.

Pour hot water to cover over the mushrooms. Set aside for 30 minutes.

Peel and devein the shrimp, and cut in half lengthwise. Toss with the cornstarch and the remaining 1 teaspoon sesame oil and set aside.

Drain the mushrooms, squeeze, cut off and discard the stems, and slice.

Combine the bok choy, bamboo, and scallions.

Combine the chicken stock, oyster sauce, light soy sauce, sugar, and salt.

(continued)

87

Heat ½ cup peanut oil in a wok or skillet to hot but not smoking. Add the shrimp, stirring to separate pieces. When barely cooked, remove to drain. Drain off the oil and reserve it.

Heat a clean wok or skillet to hot and add 2 tablespoons of the reserved oil. Add the mushroom slices, stir briefly, then add the bok choy mixture. Cook over high heat stirring vigorously to coat the vegetables with the oil. Add the chicken stock mixture and cook for another minute or so, stirring the vegetables until they wilt. Add the noodles and toss until piping hot. Add the shrimp and toss for another 30 seconds. Add the bean sprouts and toss off the heat. Serve sprinkled with the black pepper and a few drops of sesame oil.

Serves 2 if it's the whole meal, 3 to 4 as part of a larger meal

Tea-Smoked Chicken

○

This spiced, lightly smoked chicken can be eaten as you would a roast chicken; but at Big Bowl we use it only as a tasty ingredient for noodle dishes, stir-fries, soups, and salads.

2 tablespoons coarse salt

2 teaspoons Sichuan peppercorns

2 star anise

One 2-inch cinnamon stick

One 4-pound fresh chicken

1½ teaspoons dark soy sauce

FOR SMOKING

¾ cup rice

½ cup sugar

½ cup black tea

½ teaspoon sugar

Heat the salt, Sichuan peppercorns, star anise, and cinnamon sticks in a small, dry skillet over medium heat. When the seasonings begin to smoke slightly, turn off the heat. Pour the seasonings into a bowl and allow to cool.

Dry the chicken thoroughly inside and out with a paper towel. When the seasonings are cool, rub the chicken inside and out liberally with this mixture, and allow to sit on a rack where air can circulate around the chicken for 2 to 4 hours. Reserve the unused seasonings.

Bring water to boil in the bottom of a large steamer or wok. Place the chicken back side up on a rack; cover and steam for 35 minutes. Take the chicken out of the steamer and when cool enough to handle, rub thoroughly with the dark soy sauce.

Line the bottom of a large wok or heavy pot with aluminum foil. Spread the rice, sugar, and black tea over the foil. Place the chicken on a rack about 2 inches above the smoking mixture. Cover the wok or pot and use damp dish towels or paper towels to seal the crack between the pot and its cover. Turn the heat to high and when it starts to smoke, reduce the heat to medium-high and continue to cook for 15 minutes. Turn the heat off and allow the chicken to sit in the covered pot for another 40 minutes until cool. (Make sure your ventilation fan is turned on.)

At this point the chicken may be refrigerated until ready to finish, which you will do by roasting.

To roast, bring the chicken to room temperature and preheat your oven to 450 degrees.

Roast for 15 minutes until the skin browns and crisps. Meanwhile, add ½ teaspoon sugar to the leftover chicken seasonings and grind to a coarse powder in a spice grinder. When the chicken is roasted, carve and serve with the seasonings on the side.

Or you may use the smoked and roasted chicken to add its wonderful flavor to soups or noodle dishes like the Shanghai Noodles with Smoked Chicken and the Smoked Chicken Noodle Soup with Napa Cabbage that follow.

Shanghai Noodles
with Smoked Chicken

○

6 ounces fresh Shanghai noodles

1 teaspoon sesame oil plus
a few drops

¼ cup chicken stock

3 tablespoons oyster sauce

1 tablespoon light soy sauce

1 teaspoon sugar

1 tablespoon Shaoxing rice wine
or dry sherry

2 tablespoons peanut oil

½ cup sliced fresh shiitake or other
mushrooms

5 ounces sliced smoked chicken
with skin (about 1 cup)

2 scallions, cut into 2-inch lengths

1 tablespoon sliced fresh red chile
pepper (or bell pepper)

4 ounces bok choy, sliced

½ cup fresh bean sprouts

½ teaspoon freshly ground
black pepper

Bring a large quantity of unsalted water to boiling and cook the noodles as you would any pasta, about 5 minutes. Drain, run under cold water, drain again, and toss with a teaspoon of sesame oil. Set aside.

Mix together the stock, oyster sauce, light soy sauce, sugar, and rice wine; set aside.

Heat a wok or skillet over high heat and add the peanut oil. Add the mushrooms and cook until they begin to soften. Add the chicken and sauté another 30 seconds. Add the scallions, red pepper, and bok choy, and continue to cook, stirring, for 30 seconds.

Add the noodles and cook, stirring, until thoroughly hot. Add the stock mixture and cook, stirring, until the sauce is mostly reduced (add more stock if necessary). Toss in the bean sprouts and remove from the heat. Serve sprinkled with the remaining sesame oil and black pepper.

Serves 2 to 3

Smoked Chicken Noodle Soup with Napa Cabbage

○

An extraordinary hearty winter soup with a rich, smoked-chicken broth. Making the egg crepes, which add color to the soup, is optional.

4 ounces fresh Shanghai noodles

½ teaspoon sesame oil plus a few drops

EGG CREPES

1 egg

¼ teaspoon sesame oil plus a few drops for coating the pan

1 teaspoon peanut oil

3 ½ cups chicken stock

1 ½ teaspoons salt

1 teaspoon sugar

4 ounces Tea-Smoked Chicken (page 88)

¼ cup sliced bamboo shoots

½ cup sliced napa cabbage

2 tablespoons soaked and sliced dried black mushrooms

2 scallions, sliced

Black pepper

Bring a large quantity of unsalted water to a boil and cook the noodles a you would any pasta, about 5 minutes. Drain, run under cold water, drain again, and toss with ½ teaspoon of sesame oil. Set aside.

Make egg crepes (optional): Beat the egg lightly with ¼ teaspoon sesame oil. Heat a small pan or skillet till hot but not smoking and add a few drops of oil just to coat the bottom. Add a ladleful of the egg and swirl around the pan until it covers the bottom. Pour any excess back into the bowl. Cook briefly over medium heat, just until egg sets (it should not brown), and turn out onto a cutting board. Wipe the pan with an oil-dampened paper towel and repeat the process until the egg is gone. Stack the crepes, roll up, and cut into ¼-inch widths. The crepes will now have the shape of flat noodles.

Combine the chicken stock with the salt and sugar; set aside.

Heat a skillet, wok, or pot over high heat and add the peanut oil. Add the smoked chicken and cook over high heat for about 30 seconds. Add the bamboo shoots, cabbage, and mushrooms. Cook, stirring, for 1–2 minutes. Add the chicken stock and bring to a boil. Turn down the heat and simmer for 4 minutes. Divide the noodles between two soup bowls. Add the egg crepe (if used). Pour over the hot soup and serve sprinkled with black pepper and a few drops of sesame oil and garnished with the scallions.

Serves 2

Shanghai Noodles
with Pork and Napa Cabbage

○

This is a wonderful, easy-to-make version of what are typically called "Shanghai Noodles" in restaurants that offer Shanghainese specialties. Featuring golden shreds of pork and salted mustard greens or cabbage, it is the most popular way these noodles are enjoyed worldwide. The noodles achieve a golden sheen in the cooking process.

¾ pound napa cabbage or Chinese mustard greens

½ cup julienned bamboo shoots

2 teaspoons salt

½ pound pork loin, cut into julienned strips

3 tablespoons dark soy sauce

2 teaspoons sugar

8 ounces fresh Shanghai noodles

5 tablespoons plus 1 teaspoon peanut or vegetable oil

½ teaspoon sesame oil

Cut the cabbage into thin slices, combine with the bamboo shoots, and toss with the salt. Allow to sit for at least 1 hour.

Mix the pork with 2 teapoons of the dark soy sauce and set aside.

Mix the remaining dark soy sauce with the sugar.

Bring a large amount of water to boiling and cook the noodles as you would any pasta, around 5 minutes or until done. Drain, run under cold water to stop the cooking, drain again, and toss with 1 teaspoon of the peanut oil. Set aside.

Squeeze the liquid from the cabbage and bamboo shoots with your hands and set aside, discarding the liquid.

Heat a wok or skillet over high heat. When hot, add 3 tablespoons of the oil. Add the pork, stirring quickly just to separate the shreds and coat them with oil. Next add the cabbage and bamboo shoots, and cook, tossing, until they are well coated with the oil and piping hot, about 1½ minutes. Remove this cabbage-pork mixture to a bowl.

Wipe out the pan and heat again to hot. Add the remaining 2 tablespoons oil. When hot, add the noodles and toss until coated with the oil and hot. Add the soy-sugar mixture and toss the noodles until they're well coated and evenly colored. Re-add the cabbage and pork, and cook, stirring the entire dish until it's piping hot. Serve sprinkled with the sesame oil.

Serves 2 as part of a meal

North Chinese Pork and Bean Sauce with Fresh Shanghai Noodles

○

We made this topping at our annual Big Bowl Noodlefest to go with noodles that were "hand-thrown," a process where a Northern Chinese chef takes a lump of dough and stretches it out to the length of a jump rope; then he twists it, pulls it, and whaps it on a table while it divides, as if by magic, into finer and finer noodles, culminating in over 1,000.

Noodle connoisseurs in China's far north won't settle for anything but hand-thrown noodles, as they have a particular texture in the form of a discernible tension as you bite into them. Here we substitute Shanghai noodles, which are a hand-cut progeny of these noodles. This dish is traditionally served with a vinegar and chili oil mixture, and fresh bean sprouts on the side.

¼ cup red wine vinegar

2 teaspoons chili oil (see page 9)

1 cup fresh bean sprouts

2 tablespoons peanut oil

½ cup finely diced bamboo shoots

1 pound fresh Shanghai noodles

½ cup sliced scallion whites

1 pound fatty pork, ground once and lightly hand-chopped

1 teaspoon dark soy sauce

1 tablespoon chili paste with garlic

5 tablespoons bean sauce

1½ tablespoons sugar

½ cup thinly sliced scallion greens

Few drops sesame oil

Coriander sprigs for garnish

To make the accompaniments, mix together the vinegar and chili oil (don't worry, they won't combine) in a small dish to be served on the side with this noodle dish. Place the bean sprouts on a small plate and, when the noodle dish is done, provide these for each guest to help herself, sprinkling over the vinegar mixture and adding the bean sprouts to taste.

Bring a large quantity of water to boil in order to cook the noodles just before they're served.

Heat a skillet or wok over high heat. When hot, add the peanut oil, the bamboo shoots, and the scallion whites, and stir briefly to coat. Add the pork and stir, pressing the spatula down and mashing the pork to separate the grains. Do not brown. When the pork has separated and changed color, add the dark soy sauce and stir in briefly. Add the chili paste, bean sauce, and sugar, and cook, stirring, for 3 to 4 minutes. Turn off the heat (this sauce can be made hours ahead).

When the water boils, cook the noodles and drain thoroughly. Transfer to a bowl or 2 to 4 individual serving bowls. Reheat the pork, if necessary, stir in the scallion greens, and spoon the pork sauce over the noodles. Sprinkle with the sesame oil, garnish with the cilantro, and serve.

Serves 2 as a meal or 4 as part of a larger meal

Sea Scallops and
Fresh Water Chestnuts with
Ground Pork over Shanghai Noodles

○

One of the earliest recorded versions of "Meat and Spaghetti," and one still popular today is a simple Northern Chinese dish known as *za jiang mein,* or "noodles with bean sauce." A spicy version of it appears elsewhere in the book (North Chinese Pork and Bean Sauce with Fresh Shanghai Noodles, page 93). This dish adds fresh sea scallops and fresh water chestnuts, and is traditionally served with a vinegar and chili oil mixture, and fresh bean sprouts on the side.

¼ cup red wine vinegar

2 teaspoons chili oil (page 9)

1 cup fresh bean sprouts

5 ounces fresh sea scallops, cut into semicircles

1 teaspoon cornstarch

½ teaspoon plus a few drops of sesame oil

2 tablespoons peanut oil

1 cup of peanut oil

4 fresh water chestnuts, peeled, halved, and cut into semicircles

½ cup finely diced bamboo shoots

½ cup sliced scallion whites

1 pound fatty pork, ground once and lightly hand-chopped

1 teaspoon dark soy sauce

1 tablespoon chili paste with garlic

5 tablespoons bean sauce

1½ tablespoons sugar

1 pound fresh Shanghai noodles

½ cup thinly sliced scallion green

Sprigs of fresh coriander

To make the accompaniments, mix together the vinegar and chili oil (don't worry, they won't combine) in a small dish to be served on the side. Place the bean sprouts on a small plate and, when the noodle dish is done, provide these for each guest to help herself, sprinkling over the vinegar mixture and adding the bean sprouts to taste.

Bring a large quantity of water to boil in order to cook the noodles just before they're served.

Heat a wok or small pot over high heat and add the oil. When the oil is hot but not smoking, add the scallops. Cook, stirring until they just change color, and remove to a colander to drain. Strain the oil into another container and reserve.

Heat a clean skillet or wok over high heat. When hot, add 3 tablespoons of the reserved oil. Allow to heat briefly and add the water chestnuts, bamboo shoots, and scallion whites and stir briefly to coat.

Add the pork and stir, pressing down with the spatula to separate the grains. Do not brown. When the pork has separated and changed color, add the dark soy and stir in briefly. Add the chili paste, bean sauce, and sugar, and cook, stirring, for about a minute. Add the scallops and cook, stirring, until the mixture is piping hot. Turn off the heat (this sauce can be made hours ahead).

When the water boils, cook the noodles and drain thoroughly. Transfer to a bowl or 2 to 4 individual serving bowls. Reheat the pork, if necessary, stir in the scallions, and spoon the pork sauce over the noodles. Sprinkle with the sesame oil, garnish with the coriander, and serve.

Serves 2 as a main course, 4 as part of a larger meal

Shanghai Noodles
with Ground Beef, Peas, and Peanuts

○

This is inspired by a dish in *The Chinese Cookbook* by the late Virginia Lee and the late Craig Claiborne. It's simple, delicious, and, if you make it once, you'll make it a lot.

6 ounces fresh Shanghai noodles

1½ teaspoons sesame oil

1 cup peanut oil

½ cup raw (blanched and husked) peanuts

½ pound ground chuck (not too lean)

1 tablespoon dark soy sauce

1½ teaspoons sugar

3 teaspoons cornstarch

1 teaspoon salt

½ cup frozen peas

1 to 2 tablespoons dry white wine or Shaoxing rice wine

Bring a large quantity of unsalted water to boil and cook the noodles as you would any pasta, about 5 minutes. Drain, run under cold water, drain again, and toss with ½ teaspoon of sesame oil. Set aside.

Heat 1 cup peanut oil in a small pot until nearly smoking. Add the peanuts, stir gently for 20 seconds, then turn off the heat and allow to sit for 10 minutes or until the peanuts are golden. Drain the peanuts, setting them aside, and reserve the oil.

Mix the beef with the dark soy sauce, 1 teaspoon of the sugar, 1 teaspoon of the cornstarch, and the remaining 1 teaspoon sesame oil; set aside. Combine the salt and the remaining ½ teaspoon sugar with ½ cup water; stir together the remaining 2 teaspoons cornstarch and 2 tablespoons of water.

Heat a wok or skillet to hot and add 3 tablespoons of the reserved oil. When hot, add the beef and cook, stirring and mashing with a spatula to break it up, but do not brown. When the beef changes color, add the salted water and bring to a boil. Add the noodles and toss until hot and mixed with the beef. Stir in the peas and toss. Give the cornstarch/water mixture a quick stir and add it. Toss until piping hot. Add the wine, stir briefly, and serve, topped with the reserved peanuts.

Serves 2 as part of a meal

9 PAD THAI RICE NOODLES

Pad Thai with Wok-Seared Salmon

○

This is a meal unto itself. The salmon, cooked and drizzled with a sauce that is slightly more tangy than the Pad Thai noodle dish it rests on, adds some elegance to this most famous Thai noodle dish.

8 ounces (½ package) dried
  Pad Thai rice noodles

8 ounce fillet of salmon,
  preferably Wild King

1 teaspoon sesame oil

Salt

6 tablespoons fresh lime juice

3½ tablespoons brown sugar

¾ teaspoon dried red chiles,
  ground

¾ teaspoon paprika

3 tablespoons bottled Thai
  chili sauce

5½ tablespoons fish sauce

⅓ cup plus 2 tablespoons
  peanut oil

2 eggs, lightly beaten

½ cup thinly sliced scallion greens

Pour very hot tap water to cover the noodles and let sit 30 minutes. Drain well, rinse the noodles thoroughly with cold water, and set aside.

Rub the salmon with the sesame oil and sprinkle both sides with salt.

Mix two simple sauces and keep them separate: For the Pad Thai sauce, combine 4 tablespoons of the lime juice, 2 tablespoons of the brown sugar, the ground chiles, paprika, Thai chili sauce, and 3½ tablespoons of the fish sauce, and set aside. In another bowl, mix the salmon sauce: the remaining 2 tablespoons lime juice, the remaining 1½ tablespoons brown sugar, and the remaining 2 tablespoons fish sauce.

Heat a clean wok or skillet to very hot. Add ⅓ cup of oil. When very hot, add the eggs and stir quickly to set (do not brown). Push to one side of the pan and add the scallion greens. Stir briefly

2½ tablespoons Thai basil, chopped (save pinch for final garnish)

2½ tablespoons cilantro leaves (save pinch for final garnish)

1 tablespoon ground dried shrimp

3½ tablespoons chopped roasted peanuts (save ½ tablespoon for final garnish)

½ pound fresh bean sprouts

Lime wedges for garnish

½ cup fresh seasonal vegetables (snow peas, asparagus, bok choy, etc.)

just to coat with the oil, then add the noodles. Toss the noodles in the pan continually until they soften and are well coated with the oil, and the eggs and scallion greens are mixed in. When the pan is piping hot, drizzle in the Pad Thai sauce. After 5 seconds, pull the pan from the heat and toss vigorously. Add most of the basil and cilantro leaves (reserving a pinch of each for a final garnish), the dried shrimp, and the peanuts, and toss. Add the bean sprouts and keep tossing. Transfer to a warm serving plate.

Heat another pan or skillet over high heat and add 2 tablespoons oil. When hot, add the salmon and sear on one side. Turn the salmon, add ¼ cup water, and cover. Cook about 1½ to 2 minutes until medium-rare, or longer if you like (you may have to add more water).

When the salmon is done, place it on top of the Pad Thai and add the salmon sauce to the pan (the water should be almost gone). With the heat on high, reduce briefly. Turn off the heat and keep the sauce in the pan. Spoon about 1 tablespoon of the sauce over the fish, sprinkle with the basil, cilantro, and peanuts, and serve with lime wedges on the side to be used by the eaters at their discretion.

Serves 2 as a meal, 4 if part of a larger meal

Chicken Pad Thai

○

The versions of Pad Thai one gets in Thai-style fast food places and delis usually don't do justice to what the dish can be. We think this an especially clean-tasting, fresh version of a classic. And it's a little peppery.

5⅓ ounces (⅓ package) dried Pad Thai rice noodles

6 ounces boneless chicken breast, julienned

1 teaspoon cornstarch

¼ teaspoon salt

1 teaspoon sesame oil

2 tablespoons fresh lime juice

1 tablespoon brown sugar

½ teaspoon dried red chiles, ground

½ teaspoon paprika

2 tablespoons bottled Thai chili sauce

2 tablespoons fish sauce

1 cup peanut oil

1 egg, lightly beaten

⅓ cup thinly sliced scallion greens

2 tablespoons Thai basil, chopped

2 tablespoons cilantro leaves

1 tablespoon ground dried shrimp

3 tablespoons chopped roasted peanuts

1 cup fresh bean sprouts

Lime wedges for garnish

Pour very hot tap water to cover the noodles and let sit 30 minutes. Drain thoroughly, rinse with cold water, and set aside.

Mix the chicken with the cornstarch, salt, and sesame oil.

Mix together the lime juice, brown sugar, ground chiles, paprika, Thai chili sauce, and fish sauce, and set aside.

In a wok or skillet, heat 1 cup peanut oil. When hot but not smoking, add the chicken. Stir to separate the pieces. When they change color, remove to drain in a colander. Reserve the oil.

Heat a clean wok or skillet to very hot. Add 3 tablespoons of the reserved oil. When hot, add the egg, and stir quickly to set (do not brown). Push to one side of the pan and add the scallion greens. Stir briefly just to coat with the oil, then add the noodles. Toss the noodles in the pan 15 seconds or so and re-add the chicken. Toss continually until the noodles soften and are well coated with the oil, and the chicken, egg, and scallion greens are mixed in. When the pan is piping hot, drizzle in the lime juice–brown sugar mixture. After 5 seconds, pull the pan from the heat and toss vigorously. Add most of the basil and cilantro leaves (reserving a pinch of each for a final garnish), the dried shrimp, and the peanuts, and toss. Add the bean sprouts and keep tossing. Transfer to a serving plate and serve with 2 lime wedges on the side to be used by the diners at their discretion. A few drips of lime juice before one digs in are, in fact, recommended.

Serves 1 hungry person or 2 to 3 as part of a larger meal

Singapore Noodles

○

For anyone who frequents Chinese or Thai noodle shops, certain dishes—Pad Thai, Chow Fun, Chow Mein—are familiar to the point where you can make subtle distinctions between all the versions you've had. Singapore Noodles on a Chinese menu usually means deliciously oily curried rice noodles with pork. Traditionally the sweet red barbecued pork the Cantonese call *cha siu* is part of the equation.

Like all of these well-known menu staples, this dish can be excellent using the right ingredients. Here, instead of the traditional curry powder, the dish is greatly improved by using the Yellow Curry Paste we make at Big Bowl, not to mention fresh basil and freshly squeezed lemon juice.

5⅓ ounces (⅓ package) thin dried rice noodles

⅔ cup chicken stock

1 ½ tablespoons oyster sauce

1 teaspoon salt

1 teaspoon sugar

3 tablespoons peanut oil

½ cup sliced yellow onion

1 tablespoon shredded red chile pepper

2 tablespoons Yellow Curry Paste (page 16) or 1 tablespoon curry powder

¾ cup narrow slices Chinese barbecued pork (*cha siu*) (see Note), or roast pork loin

1 tablespoon Thai basil

1 tablespoon fresh lemon juice

1 cup bean sprouts

Cilantro sprigs for garnish

Soak the rice noodles in hot tap water to cover until soft; drain, rinse in cold water, and set them aside.

Combine the chicken stock, oyster sauce, salt, and sugar; set aside.

Heat a wok or skillet to hot and add the oil. When hot add the onion and chile shreds. Sauté until the onion is translucent, then add the curry paste. Stir briefly to release the flavor.

Add about half the seasoned chicken stock and, when piping hot, add the noodles. Stir briefly and add the pork. Cook, tossing, until hot and the noodles soften, and add the rest of the stock. Stir in the basil and add the lemon juice. Add the bean sprouts and immediately remove from the heat. Toss to stir in the bean sprouts, and serve garnished with the cilantro sprigs.

NOTE: For this recipe you can either prepare the Chinese Barbecued Pork Shoulder on page 23 or purchase it precooked. Chinese barbecued pork (*cha siu*) is available in Chinese markets and delicatessens, where it's cooked fresh. Reddish in color, it's displayed hanging in strips, often next to chickens, ducks, and other roast meats.

Serves 1 or 2 as a meal

Bangkok Beef Coconut Curry
Over Pad Thai Noodles

○

Served over thin rice noodles, this creamy fresh curry topped with freshly cracked pepper is simple and delicious. Its clean taste comes from our made-from-scratch Yellow Curry Paste.

6 ounces Pad Thai "rice sticks"

¾ cup canned unsweetened coconut milk

8 ounces flank steak, thinly sliced

1 teaspoon Chinese dark soy sauce

2 teaspoons cornstarch

1 teaspoon sesame oil

1 cup peanut or vegetable oil

2 tablespoons julienned fresh red hot or sweet peppers

12 to 15 fresh green or yellow beans

2 rounded tablespoons fresh Yellow Curry Paste (page 16)

⅓ cup chicken stock

½ teaspoon salt

1 tablespoon freshly squeezed lime juice mixed with 1½ teaspoons sugar

1 tablespoon fish sauce

½ teaspoon freshly cracked black pepper

Place the rice noodles in hot tap water to cover and allow to sit 15 minutes or so. When soft, but not mushy, remove to drain. Cover with cold water until ready to use.

Put the coconut milk in a saucepan and, over medium heat, reduce to about ½ cup. Set aside. Toss the beef with the soy sauce, cornstarch, and sesame oil, and set aside.

Warm a small wok or saucepan over medium-high heat and add 1 cup oil. When hot but not smoking, add the beef, and cook stirring until the meat just begins to turn color. Remove to drain; reserve the oil.

Start a pot of water boiling to reheat the noodles.

Meanwhile, heat a clean wok or skillet to hot and add 2 teaspoons of the reserved oil. Add the peppers and beans, and stir until well coated with the oil. Push the vegetables slightly to the side and add the curry paste to the pan. Cook briefly, stirring, and add the chicken stock and salt. When it boils, add the reduced coconut milk. When hot, stir in the beef. Add the sugar-lime juice mixture and the fish sauce. Stir in and remove the pan from the heat.

Dip the noodles briefly into the boiling water just to heat, shake to drain, and put them into serving bowls. Serve the beef curry over the rice noodles, sprinkled with the pepper.

Serves 3 to 4

Thai Red Curry Rice Noodles
with Lamb and Chinese Chives

Taking the time to make the wonderful fresh red curry sauce for this dish is worth it; the paste can be used elsewhere—in fried rice or soups, for example.

6 ounces dried Pad Thai rice noodles

6 ounces lamb shoulder or loin

½ tablespoon dark soy sauce

1 teaspoon sesame oil

1 teaspoon cornstarch

½ cup chicken stock

½ teaspoon kosher salt

4 teaspoons fish sauce

2 tablespoons coconut milk

1 teaspoon sugar

1 cup peanut or vegetable oil

2 tablespoons julienned fresh red
    chiles or bell peppers

20 small whole green or yellow beans

¼ cup fresh Red Curry Paste
    (page 17)

½ cup cut-up Chinese chives
    (cut into 2-inch lengths)

1 tablespoon fresh lime juice

¼ cup cilantro leaves

1 tablespoon julienned Thai basil

2 tablespoons coarsely chopped
    peanuts

Soak the rice noodles in hot tap water to cover until soft. Remove, rinse under cold water, drain, and set aside.

Slice the lamb as thinly as possible across the grain into 2-inch lengths. Mix with the soy sauce, sesame oil, and cornstarch, and set aside.

Mix the chicken stock with the salt, fish sauce, coconut milk, and sugar. Set this mixture aside.

Heat 1 cup oil in a wok or small skillet to hot but not smoking. Add the lamb and stir just to separate the slices. Remove and drain when still pink in the center; reserve the oil.

Heat a clean wok or skillet. When hot, add 2 tablespoons of the reserved oil. When the oil is hot add the chiles and green beans, and cook, tossing rapidly until just coated with the oil. Shove the vegetables aside and add the curry paste. Stir the paste around briefly just to release the flavor, and add the seasoned stock. Allow to come to a total boil and add the noodles.

Cook, stirring and tossing, until the noodles are softened and the ingredients are well mixed. Add the lamb and chives, and toss until mixed.

Add the lime juice to the noodles and toss until the whole mixture is piping hot. Remove from the heat, stir in the cilantro and basil; remove to a platter, sprinkle with the peanuts, and serve.

Serves 2 as a complete meal, 3 to 4 as part of a larger meal

"Blazing" Big Rice Noodles with Beef

I firmly believe humanity has a natural affinity for the comfort afforded by a bowl of warm noodles. However, I was initially skeptical regarding these broad, slightly glutinous rice noodles because it seemed their slippery texture, more characteristic of many Asian foods, would feel exotic to a Middle American palate. It was the dish below that proved me wrong.

From the beginning Big Bowl customers have devoured literally tons of these "big rice noodles," seasoned with salted black beans, garlic, ginger, and slices of green jalapeño—which is why they're called "blazing."

5 ounces flank steak, thinly sliced

1½ teaspoons dark soy sauce

1 teaspoon cornstarch

½ teaspoon sesame oil plus few drops for sprinkling

½ cup fresh chicken broth

2 tablespoons oyster sauce

1½ tablespoons light soy sauce

2 teaspoons red wine vinegar

1 teaspoon dark soy sauce

1½ teaspoons sugar

About 1 cup peanut or vegetable oil

14 ounces fresh "big rice noodles," sliced into ¾-inch widths

8 slices jalapeño peppers

1½ teaspoons Chinese salted black beans

2 teaspoons chopped fresh ginger

2 teaspoons chopped fresh garlic

3 tablespoons thinly sliced strips red bell or fresh chile pepper

3 scallions, cut into 2-inch lengths

5 ounces baby bok choy, quartered lengthwise

¼ cup sliced scallion greens

Freshly ground black pepper

Mix the beef with the dark soy sauce, salt, cornstarch, and the ½ teaspoon sesame oil, and set aside.

Mix ¼ cup of the broth, the oyster sauce, light soy sauce, vinegar, dark soy sauce, and sugar; set aside.

Heat about a cup of oil in a wok or skillet and when hot but not smoking, add the beef and cook, stirring, until the meat starts to change color (it should still be pink). Remove with a slotted spoon to drain. Remove the oil from the pan and reserve.

Heat a wok or skillet to hot and add 4 tablespoons of the reserved oil, and swirl the oil around the pan. When hot, add the noodles, spread out over the bottom of the pan, and let cook for 2 to 3 minutes, until lightly browned. Flip and cook for another 1 to 1½ minutes.

Push the noodles aside, and add the jalapeños, black beans, ginger, and garlic. Stir briefly, then toss with the noodles. When fragrant, add the red pepper, scallions, and bok choy, and continue to toss. Add the oyster sauce mixture and toss to coat. Re-add the beef and stir briefly. Add the remaining broth and continue to stir and cook until most of the liquid is gone. Remove to a plate and serve sprinkled with the green scallion slices, the sesame oil, and the black pepper.

Serves 2 as a complete meal, 3 to 4 as part of a larger meal

Shrimp and Chicken Chow Fun

Chow Fun" loosely means "pan-fried noodles." But as a staple of Chinese snack shops and noodle houses, it refers specifically to a slithery broad noodle, usually made of rice flour. It has a wok-scorched flavor that people love. This version calls for the fresh wide rice noodles we call "big rice noodles" at Big Bowl, here combined with shrimp and chicken breast.

15 ounces fresh Chow Fun rice noodles or one 7-ounce package ½ inch wide dried rice noodles

4 ounces boneless chicken breast, sliced

3 teaspoons cornstarch

1 teaspoon sesame oil

½ teaspoon salt

If using dried noodles, put them in a mixing bowl, cover with hot water, and let stand until softened. When ready, drain and set aside.

Put the chicken breast in small bowl and mix with 1 teaspoon of the cornstarch, ½ teaspoon of the sesame oil, and the ½ teaspoon salt. Add the shrimp to the bowl and mix in 1 teaspoon of cornstarch and the remaining teaspoon of sesame oil. Set aside.

Combine the remaining 1 teaspoon of cornstarch with 1 tablespoon water; keep handy.

Combine 2 tablespoons of the chicken stock with the oyster sauce, light soy sauce, sugar, and wine; set aside.

(continued)

4 ounces shrimp, peeled, deveined, and cut in half lengthwise

1 cup peanut oil

½ cup unseasoned chicken stock

2 tablespoons oyster sauce

1 tablespoon light soy sauce

2 teaspoons sugar

2 tablespoons Shaoxing rice wine or dry sherry

12 to 15 snow peas or sugar snap peas, stringed

¼ cup julienned fresh red chile peppers

¼ cup julienned scallion, cut into 2-inch lengths

2 teaspoons Chinese salted black beans, very lightly mashed

1 teaspoon fresh garlic

1 tablespoon fresh ginger

Freshly ground black pepper for garnish

In a wok or skillet heat 1 cup oil to hot. When hot but not smoking, add the chicken and shrimp; cook, stirring to separate the pieces. When the pieces change color, remove to a colander to drain and reserve the oil.

Heat a wok or skillet to very hot, add 4 tablespoons of the reserved oil, and swirl around the pan. When hot, add the noodles, spread out over the bottom of the pan, and let cook for 4 minutes or so, until lightly browned. Flip and cook for another 2 minutes.

Add the snow peas, chiles, and scallions, and cook, stirring, over high heat for 1 to 2 minutes. Add the black beans, garlic, and ginger, and stir briefly. Add the chicken stock–oyster sauce mixture and cook over high heat until the sauce is piping hot.

Continue to cook, stirring, over high heat and re-add the shrimp and chicken. Stir briefly and add the remaining chicken stock. When boiling, give the reserved cornstarch and water mixture a quick stir and add it. Cook, tossing, until the noodles are well coated with the sauce and shiny. Stir, and remove to a serving plate. Serve garnished with black pepper and a few drops of sesame oil.

Serves 2 as a complete meal, 3 to 4 as part of a larger meal

Burmese Seafood Chow Fun

This is a glorious, lightly curried broad noodle dish, with six kinds of fish and shellfish. Substitutes of course can be made: another fish for salmon, all clams instead of clams and mussels, etc.

12 ounces fresh Chow Fun rice noodles or one 7-ounce package ½-inch-wide dried rice noodles

1½ tablespoons fish sauce

1 tablespoon fresh lemon juice

1 teaspoon sugar

⅓ cup coconut milk

½ cup chicken stock

2 tablespoons curry paste (red or yellow, pages 17 and 16)

2 tablespoons peanut oil

¼ pound mussels, scrubbed and debearded

¼ pound clams

8 snow peas or sugar snap peas

2 tablespoons julienned fresh red chile pepper

2 to 3 sea scallops, cut in half

3 shrimp, butterflied

1 to 2 ounces salmon, thickly sliced

2 small squid, cleaned and cut into rings, tentacles cut in half

¼ cup fresh cilantro leaves for garnish

Freshly ground black pepper for garnish

If using dried noodles, put them in a mixing bowl, cover with hot water, and let stand until softened. When ready, drain and set aside.

Bring a pot of water to boil to briefly heat the noodles (fresh or dried) just before serving.

Combine the fish sauce, lemon juice, and sugar; set aside.

Put the coconut milk and ¼ cup of the stock together in a saucepan and reduce over medium heat by one-third. Heat a wok or skillet to hot. Add the oil. When hot, stir in the curry paste briefly and toss the mussels and clams. Add the snow peas and pepper and stir for 15 seconds. Add the remaining ¼ cup of chicken stock and bring to a boil. Simmer until the clams and mussels just open. Add the remaining seafood and stir just until all the pieces are separated. Mix in the coconut curry sauce and leave over low heat.

Put the Chow Fun noodles in a strainer and dip in the pot of boiling water just to reheat. Drain thoroughly and put into 3 to 4 serving bowls.

Stir the fish sauce mixture into the seafood and curry sauce, and pour over the noodles. Serve garnished with the fresh cilantro and black pepper.

Serves 3 to 4 as part of a meal

Beef Chow Fun

○

Familiar from Chinatown noodle houses, wide rice noodles are wok-cooked over tremendous heat, seared, sometimes slightly scorched, then tossed with sliced steak, Chinese salted black beans, and garlic. Their greasy goodness is usually augmented with chile pepper condiment. You won't need 100,000 BTU's of heat for this version, which we think is more refined but just as spicy, earthy, and irresistible.

15 ounces fresh Chow Fun rice noodles or one 7-ounce package ½-inch-wide dried rice noodles

6 ounces flank steak

2 teaspoons dark soy sauce

3 teaspoons cornstarch

1 teaspoon sesame oil

Peanut oil

4 ounces fresh string beans, cut on the bias into 2-inch lengths

¼ cup julienned fresh red chile peppers

½ cup julienned scallions, cut into 2-inch lengths

2 teaspoons Chinese salted black beans, very lightly mashed

2 teaspoons chopped fresh garlic

2 teaspoons chopped fresh ginger

½ cup unseasoned chicken stock

2 tablespoons oyster sauce

1 tablespoon light soy sauce

2 teaspoons sugar

1 tablespoon Shaoxing rice wine or dry sherry

Freshly ground black pepper for garnish

If you are using dried noodles, put the noodles in a mixing bowl, cover with hot water, and let stand until softened. When ready, drain and set aside.

Slice the beef thinly across the grain and mix with the dark soy sauce, 2 teaspoons of the cornstarch, and the sesame oil.

Mix ¼ cup of the chicken stock with the oyster sauce, light soy sauce, sugar, and wine; set aside.

Mix the remaining teaspoon of cornstarch with 1 tablespoon water.

Heat 1 cup oil in a wok or skillet until the oil is hot but not smoking. Add the beef and cook, stirring just to separate the pieces. Remove to drain in a colander when medium-rare. Pour off the oil and reserve.

Heat a wok or skillet to hot, add 4 tablespoons of the reserved oil, and swirl around the pan. When hot, add the noodles, spread out over the bottom of the pan, and let cook for 4 minutes or so, until lightly browned. Flip and cook for another 2 minutes.

Add the green beans, chile, and scallions, and cook, stirring, over high heat for 1 to 2 minutes. Add the black beans, garlic, and ginger, and toss briefly. Add the chicken stock–oyster sauce mixture and cook over high heat until the sauce is piping hot.

Continue to cook, stirring, over high heat and re-add the beef. Stir briefly and add the remaining chicken stock. When boiling, give the cornstarch and water mixture a quick stir and add it. Cook, tossing, until the noodles are well coated with the sauce and are shiny. Serve garnished with black pepper and a few drops of sesame oil.

Serves 2 as a complete meal, 3 to 4 as part of a larger meal

Chow Fun with Chinese Barbecued Pork and Snow Peas

○

A hearty, satisfying noodle dish with great flavor that is reminiscent of the best in Chinese-American cooking. It's well worth making Chinese Barbecued Pork Shoulder (page 23) just for this colorful dish.

15 ounces fresh Chow Fun rice noodles or one 7-ounce package ½-inch-wide dried rice noodles)

½ cup unseasoned chicken stock

2 tablespoons oyster sauce

1 tablespoon light soy sauce

2 teaspoons sugar

1 tablespoon Shaoxing rice wine or dry sherry

¼ cup peanut oil

4 ounces fresh snow peas

½ cup scallions, cut into 2-inch lengths and julienned

8 ounces barbecued pork , thinly sliced

2 teaspoons finely chopped fresh garlic

2 teaspoon finely chopped fresh ginger

½ teaspoon cornstarch mixed with 2 teaspoons water

½ cup bean sprouts

Freshly ground black pepper

Few drops of sesame oil

If using dried noodles, put noodles in a mixing bowl, cover with hot water, and let stand until softened. When ready, drain and set aside.

Mix ¼ cup of the chicken stock with the oyster sauce, light soy sauce, sugar, and wine; set aside.

Heat a wok or skillet over high heat, add the ¼ of oil and swirl around the pan. When the oil is hot, add the noodles, spread them out over the bottom of the pan, and let cook for 4 minutes or so, until lightly browned. Flip and cook for another 2 minutes.

Add the snow peas and scallions and cook, tossing, over high heat for 1–2 minutes. Add the pork, garlic, and ginger and toss briefly. Add the chicken stock–oyster sauce mixture and cook, tossing over high heat until the sauce is piping hot.

Continue to cook, stirring, over high heat and add the remaining chicken stock. When boiling, give the cornstarch and water mixture a quick stir to recombine, and add it. Cook, tossing, until the noodles are shiny and well coated with the sauce. Add the bean sprouts and pull the pan off the heat as you toss to mix them in. Serve garnished with black pepper and a few drops of sesame oil.

Serves 2 as a main course, 3 to 4 as part of a larger meal

RICE DISHES

We recommend that all the following dishes be accompanied by freshly cooked rice except where specified. At Big Bowl we use a superior grade of long-grain Thai jasmine rice.

Spring Asparagus with Chicken Stir-Fry

Rare in Chinese restaurants, this springtime dish should thrill anyone who encounters it. Its colorful and wonderfully earthy combination of fresh shiitake, Chinese salted black beans, and fresh asparagus should become one of the most frequently made recipes in this book. Another equally delicious version made with egg noodles appears on page 78.

8 ounces boneless chicken breast, sliced

2 teaspoons cornstarch

1 teaspoon sesame oil plus few drops sesame oil

2 tablespoons oyster sauce

1 tablespoon light soy sauce

1 teaspoon sugar

½ cup chicken stock

1 cup peanut oil

3 small fresh shiitake mushrooms, sliced

1 teaspoon Chinese salted black beans

2 teaspoons julienned fresh red chile pepper

2 teaspoons chopped fresh ginger

2 teaspoons chopped fresh garlic

½ pound fresh asparagus, trimmed and cut on the bias into 2-inch lengths

2 teaspoons cornstarch mixed into 2 tablespoons water

Mix the chicken with the cornstarch and sesame oil, and set aside.

Combine the oyster sauce, light soy sauce, sugar, and chicken stock; set aside.

Heat 1 cup oil in a wok or skillet to hot and add the chicken. Cook, stirring, just until the chicken turns color. Remove to drain; reserve the oil.

Heat a wok or skillet over high heat. When hot, add 3 tablespoons of the reserved oil. Add the mushroom slices and cook, stirring, until browned lightly and soft. Add the black beans, chile pepper, ginger, and garlic, and cook, stirring. Add the asparagus and toss until well coated with the seasonings. Add the oyster sauce mixture and bring to a boil. Re-add the chicken and cook, tossing, until it heats. When the sauce boils, re-stir the cornstarch mixture and add. Cook over high heat until the sauce thickens slightly and clears.

Remove to a serving bowl and sprinkle with sesame oil. Serve with plain rice.

Serves 2 with rice as a complete meal, 3 to 4 as part of a larger meal

Summer Chicken
with Fresh-Shucked Corn and Peas

○

An American-sounding, even Midwestern-sounding dish, this nevertheless applies Chinese cooking techniques and seasonings to fresh-shucked corn and peas, and the result is popular and tasty.

2 to 3 ears fresh sweet corn

½ pound fresh peas in the shell (should yield ¼ cup)

2 teaspoons oyster sauce

1 teaspoon light soy sauce

1 teaspoon sugar

1¼ teaspoons kosher salt

¾ cup chicken stock

6 ounces boneless chicken breast, cut into ½-inch cubes

3½ teaspoons cornstarch

1½ teaspoons sesame oil

2 cups peanut or vegetable oil

3 to 4 fresh shiitake or oyster mushrooms (or other fresh mushrooms), sliced

1 fresh red chile pepper, seeded and sliced

2 teaspoons chopped garlic

2 tablespoons Shaoxing rice wine or dry sherry

½ teaspoon freshly ground black pepper

Husk and, with a knife, cut the corn kernels off the cob into a mixing bowl.

Shell the peas into the bowl, and set aside.

Mix the oyster sauce, soy sauce, sugar, 1 teaspoon of the salt, and the chicken stock; set aside.

Mix the chicken breast with 2 teaspoons of the cornstarch, the remaining ¼ teaspoon salt, and 1 teaspoon of the sesame oil; set aside. Mix the remaining 1½ teaspoons of cornstarch with 2 tablespoons water, and set aside.

Heat 2 cups peanut oil in a wok or skillet until hot but not smoking. Add the chicken and stir, separating the pieces, just until the chicken changes color. Remove from the oil with a slotted spoon to drain.

Remove all the oil from the wok or skillet and reserve; wipe the pan and reheat over high heat. When hot, add 4 tablespoons of the reserved oil. Turn the heat to medium and add the mushrooms and chile pepper. Cook, stirring, for 1 to 2 minutes, until the mushrooms are softened. Add the garlic and stir briefly; add the corn and peas, and cook, stirring, over high heat for 30 seconds to 1 minute. Add the chicken stock mixture, bring to a boil, turn the heat to medium, and simmer until the corn and peas are cooked, about 2 minutes; re-add the chicken.

Turn the heat to high. Re-stir the cornstarch-water mixture and add. Stir over high heat until the sauce thickens and clears. Splash in the wine and continue to stir briefly. Spoon into a serving bowl or platter and serve sprinkled with sesame oil and the black pepper, accompanied by white rice.

Serves 2 with rice as a complete meal, 3 to 4 as part of a larger meal

Big Bowl Fall/Winter Chicken

The fall/winter dish features Chinese broccoli (*gai lan*), which is one of the world's most nutritious greens, especially high in calcium and vitamins A and C.

5 ounces Chinese broccoli, sliced on the bias into 3-inch sections, with leaves and flowers

2 tablespoons oyster sauce

1 tablespoon Chinese light soy sauce

1½ teaspoons sugar

1 tablespoon Shaoxing rice wine or dry sherry

½ teaspoon salt

½ cup chicken stock

6 ounces boneless chicken breast, sliced

1 teaspoon cornstarch

½ teaspoon sesame oil plus few drops for sprinkling

2 cups peanut or vegetable oil

3 to 4 fresh shiitake, oyster, or other fresh mushrooms, sliced

1½ tablespoons chopped ginger

2 teaspoons chopped garlic

2 teaspoons cornstarch blended with 2 tablespoons water

Freshly ground black pepper for garnish

Heat a pot of water to boiling and blanch the Chinese broccoli for 1 to 2 minutes. Run under cold water and drain.

Mix the oyster sauce, light soy sauce, sugar, wine, ¼ teaspoon of the salt, and the chicken stock, and set aside.

Mix the chicken with 1 teaspoon cornstarch, the remaining ¼ teaspoon salt, and ½ teaspoon sesame oil.

Heat 2 cups peanut oil in a wok or skillet until hot but not smoking. When hot add the chicken and stir, separating the pieces, just until the chicken changes color. Remove from the oil with a slotted spoon to drain.

Remove all the oil from the wok or skillet and reserve; wipe the pan and reheat over high heat. When hot, add 3 tablespoons of the reserved oil. Turn the heat to medium and add the mushrooms. Cook, stirring for 2 minutes, until the mushrooms are softened; add the ginger and garlic, and stir until fragrant. Add the broccoli, stir briefly, and re-add the chicken.

Turn the heat to high, add the sauce mixture, and bring to a boil. Re-stir the cornstarch-water mixture and add. Stir until the sauce thickens and clears. Put on a serving dish and sprinkle with sesame oil and black pepper. Serve accompanied by white rice.

Serves 2 with rice as a complete meal, 3 to 4 as part of a larger meal

Thai Red Curry Chicken
with Wrinkled Yellow Beans

○

This is a great spicy summer dish that's pretty foolproof. The beans here are first cooked briefly in very hot oil, which "wrinkles" them, giving them a soft, sweet taste and texture, almost those of another vegetable. The curry paste and fresh chiles make it hot.

6 ounces boneless chicken breast, sliced

1 teaspoon cornstarch

¼ teaspoon salt

Sesame oil

1 tablespoon fish sauce

2 teaspoons fresh lime juice

1 teaspoon sugar

2 cups peanut oil

6 ounces fresh yellow wax beans, whole and free of moisture

½ cup sliced red onion

2 tablespoons julienned fresh red chile pepper

3 garlic cloves, smashed

2 rounded tablespoons Red Curry Paste (page 17)

¼ cup chicken stock

¼ cup sliced scallion greens

Mix the chicken with the cornstarch, salt, and sesame oil, and set aside.

Mix the fish sauce, lime juice, and sugar; set aside.

Heat the peanut oil in a wok or small skillet. When hot but not smoking, add the chicken and cook until the meat changes color. Remove to drain in a colander.

Turn the heat to high under the oil. When very hot, add the beans and cook just until they wrinkle, about 1 to 2 minutes. Remove to drain. Reserve the oil.

Heat a clean wok or skillet until hot. Add 3 tablespoons of the reserved oil and add the onion. Cook, stirring, until the onion is translucent. Add the chile pepper and stir, then the garlic. Cook, stirring, briefly. Add the curry paste and stir. Then add the chicken stock. When hot, add the chicken and beans. Toss just until hot, 20 seconds, then add the fish sauce–lime juice mixture. Toss in the scallion greens, stir, and serve with hot rice.

Serves 3 to 4 with rice as part of a large meal

Chicken with
Summer Tomatoes and Peas

○

When introduced to China from the New World about four centuries ago, tomatoes, unlike, say, peanuts or chile peppers, never caught on in a big way. They can be found there, however, and in this great summer dish, the fresh ginger and fresh water chestnuts of that ancient civilization seem made to go with just-picked red ripe tomatoes.

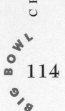
¼ cup shelled fresh peas

8 ounces boneless chicken breast, cut into ½-inch cubes

2 teaspoons cornstarch

1½ teaspoons salt

1 teaspoon sesame oil

1½ pounds red ripe tomatoes, peeled and seeded

Peanut oil

1 tablespoon sugar

2 tablespoons finely chopped ginger

1 tablespoon finely chopped garlic

⅓ cup fresh water chestnuts, peeled and cut in half

Parboil the peas in boiling water to cover for 2 minutes, drain, run under cold water to stop the cooking, and drain again.

Mix the chicken with the cornstarch, ½ teaspoon of the salt, and the sesame oil, and set aside.

Cut the tomatoes into quarters if small; if large cut them into eighths.

Heat a wok or skillet until nearly smoking. Add 2 tablespoons of the peanut oil. When hot, add the tomatoes (watch out for the splattering). Cook over high heat, stirring, and add the remaining 1 teaspoon of salt and the sugar. Cook over high heat for 3 or 4 minutes, until the tomatoes just start to soften and the sauce thickens slightly. Remove to a bowl, stir in another tablespoon of oil, and set aside.

Heat 1 cup of peanut oil in a wok or skillet until hot but not smoking. Add the chicken and cook, stirring, just until the meat turns color. Remove the chicken to a colander to drain and reserve the oil.

Heat a clean wok or skillet over high heat. When hot, add 2 tablespoons of the reserved peanut oil. When the oil is hot, add the ginger and garlic, and stir briefly. Add the fresh water chestnuts and peas, and continue to stir for about 20 seconds. Pour in the reserved tomato sauce. When combined and boiling, add the chicken; stir just to heat and serve with rice as an accompaniment.

Serves 3 to 4 with rice as part of a larger meal

Chicken with Snow Peas and Mushrooms

○

A familiar menu item perhaps, but this colorful version with two kinds of peas, the coconut crunch of fresh water chestnuts, a sauce of fresh chicken stock spiked with ginger and garlic, and a splash of the sherry-like Shaoxing rice wine, is anything but mundane.

4 medium black mushrooms

6 ounces boneless chicken breast, sliced

1 teaspoon cornstarch

1¼ teaspoons salt

½ teaspoon sesame oil plus few drops for sprinkling

½ cup chicken stock

2 teaspoons oyster sauce

2 teaspoons light soy sauce

1 teaspoon salt

1½ teaspoons sugar

1 cup peanut or vegetable oil

1 teaspoon chopped ginger

2 teaspoons chopped garlic

4 fresh water chestnuts, peeled and sliced

12 to 15 snow peas or sugar snap peas, strings removed

¼ cup fresh or frozen peas

2 teaspoons cornstarch blended with 2 tablespoons water

1 tablespoon Shaoxing rice wine or dry sherry

Black pepper for garnish

Cover the mushrooms with hot water and let sit for 30 minutes or until soft. When ready, remove from the liquid, squeeze out a little of the water, and slice; set aside.

Mix the chicken with the cornstarch, ¼ teaspoon of the salt, and ½ teaspoon sesame oil.

Mix the chicken stock with the oyster sauce, the light soy sauce, the remaining 1 teaspoon salt, and the sugar.

Heat 1 cup peanut oil in a wok or skillet until hot but not smoking. When hot add the chicken and stir, separating the pieces, just until the chicken changes color Remove from the oil with a slotted spoon to drain.

Remove all the oil from the wok or skillet (and reserve), wipe the pan, and reheat over high heat. When hot, add 4 tablespoons of the reserved peanut oil. Add the mushrooms and cook, stirring, for 15 seconds, then add the ginger, garlic, and water chestnuts, and stir briefly. Add the snow peas and peas, and stir for another 30 seconds.

Add the chicken stock mixture, bring to a boil, and re-add the chicken. Re-stir the cornstarch-water mixture and add. Stir until the sauce thickens and clears. Put on a plate and serve sprinkled with a little sesame oil and black pepper, accompanied with steaming white rice.

Serves 2 with rice as a complete meal, 3 to 4 as part of a larger meal

Fiery Hunan Chicken

This dish is the essence of Hunan/Sichuan flavors and heat. The sauce uses both fresh chiles and a garlicky, winy chili paste.

6 ounces boneless chicken breast,
 finely shredded

3 teaspoons cornstarch

1 teaspoon salt

1 teaspoon sesame oil plus
 ½ teaspoon for garnish

2 tablespoons light soy sauce

2 tablespoons chili paste with garlic

2 teaspoons sugar

1 tablespoon Shaoxing rice wine
 or dry sherry

¼ cup chicken stock

1 cup peanut or vegetable oil

2 tablespoons dried black mushrooms,
 soaked, drained, and julienned

¼ cup julienned fresh red chile
 peppers

2 tablespoons julienned bamboo
 shoots

2 tablespoons finely shredded ginger

1 tablespoon julienned carrot

5 garlic cloves, smashed

Mix the chicken shreds with 2 teaspoons of the cornstarch, ½ teaspoon of the salt, and 1 teaspoon of the sesame oil; set aside.

Mix the soy sauce, chili paste, sugar, wine, and chicken stock together.

Mix the remaining 1 teaspoon cornstarch with 1 tablespoon water.

In a wok or small skillet, heat the peanut oil to hot but not smoking. When hot, add the chicken shreds and stir until the shreds separate and change color. Remove to drain in a colander, reserving the oil.

Heat a clean wok or skillet to hot and add 3 to 4 tablespoons of the reserved oil. When the oil is hot, add the mushrooms and sauté for 30 seconds over high heat. Then add the chile peppers, bamboo shoots, ginger, carrot, and garlic, and cook, stirring, for 1 minute or so, just until the vegetables soften slightly. Add the chicken shreds and stir to combine. Then stir in the soy sauce/chili paste mixture and bring to a boil. When hot, give the cornstarch and water mixture a stir and add it. Cook, stirring, until the dish glazes, about 30 seconds. Serve garnished with the remaining ½ teaspoon of sesame oil and with rice on the side.

Serves 3 to 4 as part of a larger meal

Five Spice Whole Chicken
with Sticky Rice Packages

○

This is one of the world's juiciest and most flavorful whole chicken dishes. Two cooking processes are applied: steaming and roasting.

¼ cup kosher salt

1 teaspoon Sichuan peppercorns

2 star anise

One 1-inch stick Chinese cinnamon (cassia)

6 whole cloves

½ teaspoon cumin seeds

One 3½- to 4-pound fresh chicken, room temperature

1 teaspoon sugar

1 teaspoon dark soy sauce

4 Sticky Rice Packages (see recipe on page 118)

Heat a small skillet over medium-high heat and add the salt, peppercorns, star anise, cassia, cloves, and cumin. Cook, shaking the pan until the spices begin to smoke. Remove the pan from the heat and allow to cool.

Rub 2 tablespoons of this mixture over the chicken, inside and out, reserving the rest. Let sit for 3 hours.

To make seasoned salt, pluck any remaining large spice pieces from the spice mixture (cassia, star anise, cloves), put them in a spice grinder, and grind briefly. Add the remaining salt and spices, and grind to a coarse powder (not too fine). Remove to a bowl and stir in 1 teaspoon sugar. Serve in small dip bowls to accompany the chicken.

Pour water into a large steamer and bring to boiling. When boiling rapidly, place the chicken on a rack inside the steamer, cover, and steam over high heat for 20 minutes. Remove, and when cool enough to handle, rub the soy sauce evenly over the chicken.

If serving the chicken the same day, the chicken can sit covered until ready to roast. If cooking the next day, refrigerate, but bring the chicken to room temperature before roasting.

When ready to serve, preheat the oven to 475 degrees.

Cut the chicken in half. Remove and discard the back bone and breast bones, and lay the two halves breast side up on a sheet pan. Roast the chicken until golden, 10 to 12 minutes. Pull out of the oven and allow to rest while you steam the Sticky Rice Packages for 15 minutes.

When ready to serve, cut between the leg and thigh; cut the thigh in two pieces and the breast in three pieces. Arrange the chicken back into the two-dimensional shape you roasted it in. Serve with the Sticky Rice Packages and seasoned salt.

Serves 4

Chinese Sticky Rice Packages

○

Once made, it's not necessary to steam this rice inside lotus leaves, but doing so lends authenticity and fine flavor. This is a great accompaniment to any roast bird, which, in China, means duck, chicken, or goose. It makes an excellent Thanksgiving stuffing, by the way. (The rice will have to be soaked in cold water for 8 hours or overnight before cooking.)

If serving the packages with one roast chicken on page 117, you will need about four, reserving any leftover rice to be part of a future meal.

1¾ pounds Chinese sticky (glutinous) rice (we prefer Koda Farms)

½ cup dried black mushrooms

4 Chinese sweet sausages (*lop chong*)

¾ cup dried shrimp (large)

½ cup peanut oil

1½ cups sliced scallions, green and white

2 teaspoons kosher salt

1 teaspoon sesame oil

2 teaspoons black pepper

1 package dried lotus leaves

Rinse the glutinous rice and soak it in cold water to cover for 8 hours or overnight.

Soak the mushrooms in hot water to cover and allow to sit for 1 hour.

Drain the rice. Spread it over the bottom of a heatproof plate.

Put water in the bottom of a steamer large enough to hold the rice plate, and bring to a boil. Put the plated rice in the steamer, cover, and steam for about 30 to 40 minutes, sprinkling the rice with a little water from time to time. The rice should be soft and chewy when done, not mushy. Set aside.

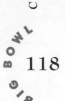

Put a little water in the bottom of a saucepan, add the sausages, cover, and steam for 10 minutes. Remove them, slice thinly on the bias, and set aside.

Remove the mushrooms from their soaking water. Squeeze out the liquid and reserve it. Cut the stems off the mushrooms and discard. Slice the mushrooms.

Using a blender, food processor, or heavy knife, chop the dried shrimp to a coarse powder.

Heat a wok or skillet to hot and add the peanut oil. When hot, add the scallions and stir briefly. Add the mushroom slices and continue to stir. Stir in the sausage, then add the rice. Cook, stirring, to mix and separate the grains by mashing them down with the spatula. Add the dried shrimp and ¼ cup of the reserved mushroom-soaking liquid. Add the salt and pepper and continue stirring. When thoroughly mixed, the dish is done. If dry when cooking, add a little more soaking liquid. Drizzle over the sesame oil.

Soak the lotus leaves in warm water until soft. Drain, add about 1 cup of the mixture to each leaf and fold. (This may be done ahead.) Steam for 10 minutes, or until hot. To serve, these may simply be unwrapped, or the top can be cut crosswise with a knife and the package can be squeezed so this top will open exposing the rice.

Makes about 8 cups

Clay Pot of Whole Chicken with Chinese Sausage and Napa Cabbage

○

This is the kind of delicious home-style Chinese dish that is rarely prepared in restaurants. At Big Bowl we serve this as well as the Shanghai Braised Clay-Pot Duck with Pearl Onions (page 121) on special occasions. A whole chicken, cut into pieces, is browned and then steamed in a wonderful wine sauce with Chinese sweet sausage (*lop chong*) and napa cabbage.

1 whole chicken, 3½ to 4 pounds, cut into 10–12 pieces, with skin

1 teaspoon kosher salt

¼ cup peanut oil

2 pounds napa cabbage, cut in half and then in 1-inch-wide slices

2 Chinese sweet sausages, sliced thinly on a bias

SAUCE

2 tablespoons Shaoxing rice wine

1 teaspoon salt

2 teaspoons sugar

2 tablespoons dark soy sauce

1 tablespoon cornstarch

1 tablespoon sesame oil

Sprinkle the chicken pieces with the salt and let them sit for 30 minutes. Heat a large, heavy skillet or wok over high heat. When hot add the oil. Brown the chicken pieces 4 or 5 at a time and remove leaving the oil. Continue until all the pieces are done. (You may have to turn the heat down if they brown too quickly.)

Add the cabbage to the same pot and cook, stirring until the cabbage reduces by half. This should take a few minutes.

Put the cabbage at the bottom of a large, heatproof casserole or Chinese clay pot. Mix together the sauce ingredients and, in a large mixing bowl, mix this sauce with the chicken pieces. Then arrange these pieces in the casserole on top of the cabbage, pouring in every drop of the sauce. Arrange the Chinese sausage slices on top of the chicken.

Bring water to a boil in the bottom of a large steamer (this may be a wok with a rack). Put the casserole in the top of the steamer, cover, and steam for 20 minutes. Uncover and serve with plain rice.

NOTE: This may be baked, covered, in a 350-degree oven for 20–25 minutes.

Serves 2 to 3 as a main meal, 3 to 4 as part of a larger meal

Roast Duck with Ginger-Orange Glaze

○

Chinese typically apply two cooking methods to a duck; one steams away the fat, which, as it melts, tenderizes the meat; the second technique, roasting, crisps the skin. Serve with the Sticky Rice Packages on page 118.

1 whole duck, about 5 pounds

3 tablespoons kosher salt

1 teaspoon Sichuan peppercorns

2 star anise

One 2-inch stick cinnamon or
    Chinese cinnamon (cassia)

¼ cup julienned ginger

Zest of 2 oranges, julienned

2 fresh red chili peppers, julienned

4 teaspoons dark soy sauce

3 tablespoons light soy sauce

⅓ cup honey

⅓ cup dark corn syrup

3 tablespoons sugar

3 tablespoons fresh lemon juice

Coriander sprigs for garnish

At least 4 hours before cooking, rinse the duck inside and out, and dry thoroughly. If cold, allow the duck to come to room temperature, about an hour, and dry again.

In a small skillet, heat the salt, peppercorns, star anise, and cinnamon, and stir over high heat until the seasonings begin to smoke. Turn off the heat and, when the seasonings are cool enough to handle, rub the duck inside and out with 2 tablespoons of the mixture, discarding the rest. Allow the duck to sit 3 hours or longer in a cool, airy place.

To make the glaze, simply put all the remaining ingredients (except the cilantro garnish) in a saucepan and cook over medium-high heat until syrupy. Transfer the sauce to a mixing bowl and allow to cool.

Bring water to boiling in the bottom of a large steamer. Put the duck, back side up, in the top of the steamer and steam over high heat for 50 to 60 minutes (you may have to add more water to the steamer). You also may steam the duck on a rack in the top of a large covered wok. When done, the wing meat should be pulling away from the bone. Allow to cool.

With a heavy French chef's knife or cleaver, split the duck in two. Remove the back bone and discard, and remove the rib bones from each half, taking care not to damage the breast.

Preheat the oven to 450 degrees.

Place the duck, skin side up, on a sheet tray or baking sheet with edges to catch any juice, and brush liberally with the honey-lemon syrup.

Roast the duck for 10 to 12 minutes until golden. Remove the duck and immediately brush again with the honey-lemon syrup. Allow to sit for 5 to 10 minutes. Then cut the duck as follows: Cut off the wings at the joints. Cut off the legs and thighs.

Separate the legs from the thighs. Cut the breast in three slices. As best you can, arrange the duck on a large platter in the same two-dimensional shape it was in when you roasted it. Serve with Sticky Rice Packages if you want, and garnish with cilantro sprigs.

NOTE: Rather than roasting, you may grill this duck on a backyard barbecue following the same basic procedure, but you need to turn it once or twice.

Serves 4 as part of a larger meal

Shanghai Braised Clay-Pot Duck with Pearl Onions

○

This succulent duck with onions could well be a casserole dish from Southwest France. It is browned and slow-cooked until it nearly falls off of the bone. The sauce, seasoned with wine, dark soy sauce, and a little yellow rock sugar has the wonderful flavors of the duck itself and of the golden browned onions that have also braised in the sauce.

Here the duck is cooked and then divided among two small Chinese "clay pot" casseroles (this can be done up to a day ahead). Either one or both can be simply steamed and served with rice and a vegetable. You will need a large vessel for initially browning the duck in oil—a 16-inch wok works nicely.

1 whole duck, 4½ to 5 pounds

2 teaspoons kosher salt

12–14 medium pearl onions (1-inch, not the tiny ones), peeled

Oil for frying

⅓ cup Shaoxing rice wine

2 lumps yellow rock sugar, approximately 1¼-inch cubes (2⅔ ounces if you have a digital scale)

¼ cup dark soy sauce

Cilantro for garnish

2 small Chinese clay pots, about 6½ inches in diameter at the top, with lids (optional)

Bring the duck to room temperature. Rinse it inside and out and dry it thoroughly inside and out. Sprinkle 1 teaspoon of the salt over the duck and inside the cavity, and let it sit on a rack in an airy place for 1 hour (it must be thoroughly dry before browning, or it will spatter in the hot oil).

In a wok or pot large enough to hold the duck, bring 6–8 cups of oil to 375 degrees. Add the onions and brown for a minute or so (they shouldn't really cook). Remove them with a skimmer or slotted spoon to a bowl; leave the hot oil in the wok.

(continued)

Carefully lower the duck into the oil. As it browns on one side, spoon the hot oil all over it to brown the skin. After 6 to 8 minutes, carefully turn the duck in the oil and repeat on the other side, again taking care to watch for spattering oil. When the duck is a light golden brown, remove to drain. The oil may be strained and stored in a light-proof container for another use.

Bring 4 cups of water to a boil. Meanwhile, heat another cooking vessel or wok large enough for the duck (you may clean and reuse the first pot) over high heat. When hot, add the Shaoxing wine. Immediately add the duck. Rotating the pan as best you can, and turning the duck, let the hot wine splash over most of the skin of the duck. With the duck back side up, pour the boiling water over it; it should be mostly covered.

Turn the heat to low, cover, and allow the duck to simmer for 15 minutes. Uncover, turn the duck over, and add the rock sugar, soy sauce, and the remaining teaspoon of salt. Cover and simmer for another 25 minutes. Add the reserved onions and simmer for another 20 minutes.

Uncover and remove the duck, leaving the liquid in the pan; allow it to cool. Reduce the liquid over high heat to about 1⅔ cups of sauce. Turn off the heat.

When the duck is cool enough to handle, split it in half lengthwise with a French chef's knife or cleaver. Remove and discard the ribs from the duck and cut each half into 6–7 pieces. Spoon the onions into the bottom of each casserole and arrange the duck pieces on top, dividing the duck between the two pots. Pour the reduced sauce over the duck, dividing it between the pots. Cover and refrigerate unless you're going to serve them within 4 hours. Bring to room temperature before continuing.

To serve, put the covered pot in a large, rapidly boiling steamer and cook for 10 minutes or until piping hot. These also may be heated in a 350-degree oven for 10–15 minutes or until hot. Serve with white rice.

Each clay pot will serve two people as part of a larger meal

12 SEAFOOD

Simple Ginger Scallion Sauce for Fresh Fish, Three Ways

○

Fresh fish with scallions and ginger is a simple but heavenly match, which is why Chinese fish dealers sometimes include a piece of ginger and a scallion or two in your bag if you buy a whole fish. Those two complementary staples heighten the fresh flavors and dampen any fishiness in even the freshest of fish. This sauce works with any kind of fish and, if you can find a whole, recently expired fish, it's particularly good. Here are three ways of using this sauce:

STEAMED FISH

One 8-ounce fish fillet of any kind or 1¼-pound whole fish, cleaned and scaled

½ teaspoon sesame oil

Kosher salt

1 tablespoon Shaoxing rice wine or other dry white wine

1 tablespoon light soy sauce

½ teaspoon sugar

¼ cup chicken stock

¼ cup peanut oil

¼ cup finely julienned ginger

⅓ cup finely julienned scallion

¼ cup cilantro leaves for garnish

Rub the fish fillet with the sesame oil and sprinkle both sides lightly with kosher salt. If using a whole fish, rinse, dry, then lightly score the skin at 2-inch intervals; rub with the sesame oil and salt lightly inside and out.

Mix the wine, soy sauce, sugar, and chicken stock, and set aside.

Pour water into the bottom of a steamer and bring to boiling; place the fish on a heatproof plate, put it in the top of a steamer, and cover. When the fish is almost done (5 minutes for the fillet and 10 minutes for the whole fish), heat a skillet to very hot. Add the peanut oil. When smoking, add the ginger and scallion. Stir very briefly, then splash in the wine-stock mixture, and remove from the heat, but leave in the pan.

BIG BOWL

When the fish is done (about 5 to 6 minutes for the fillet and 10 to 12 minutes for the whole fish), transfer the fish to a serving platter. Pour the sauce over the fish and serve garnished with the cilantro leaves.

GRILLED FISH

Simply follow the same procedure as above, rubbing a little more oil on the fish. Make sure you cook the fish on a hot grill that has been brushed with oil so the fish doesn't stick. (A whole fish may be wrapped in aluminum foil.)

"WOK-SEARED" AND STEAMED FISH

Using the ingredients above (except the chicken stock), follow the same procedure for oiling and salting the fish. Heat a wok or skillet large enough to accommodate the fish over high heat. When smoking hot, add the oil. When hot, add the fish, skin side down, and sear.

Push the fish slightly aside in the pan and add the ginger and scallion. Sauté briefly, then turn the fish over and add ⅓ cup water to the pan. Cover and cook over medium-high. When the fish is done, transfer it to a serving platter. Add the seasoned wine-soy mixture (remember this version has no chicken stock), bring briefly to a boil, and turn off the heat. Stir the cilantro leaves into the sauce, pour over the fish, and serve.

Serves 2 as part of a larger meal

Kung Pao Fish,
"Wok-Seared" and Steamed

○

This tangy-sweet and fiery reddish sauce works as a wonderful complement to any delicate, white-fleshed fish such as halibut or sea bass.

2 tablespoons peanut oil

One 8-ounce fish fillet (halibut or other white-fleshed fish)

1 tablespoon finely julienned bamboo shoots

2 tablespoons finely julienned fresh ginger

1 tablespoon julienned fresh red chile pepper

KUNG PAO SAUCE

1 tablespoon red wine vinegar

2 teaspoons light soy sauce

½ teaspoon Chinese dark soy sauce

2 teaspoons chili paste with garlic

2 teaspoons hoisin sauce

1 teaspoon sugar

1 tablespoon Shaoxing rice wine

½ cup fresh cilantro leaves

½ teaspoon sesame oil

Heat the pan or skillet to nearly smoking and add the peanut oil. When hot, sear the fish skin side down. Add the bamboo, ginger, and chile and stir these vegetables briefly. Add the Kung Pao Sauce and stir briefly. Turn the fish, add the water, and cover.

Steam the fish for a couple of minutes, or until nearly done. Uncover and continue to cook to reduce the sauce (there should be some sauce left; it should not be a glaze). Take the pan off the heat. Remove the fish with a slotted spoon to a serving plate. Add the cilantro leaves to the sauce and stir in until wilted. Pour over the fish. Sprinkle with the sesame oil. Serve with rice and vegetables of your choice.

Serves 2 as part of a larger meal

Alaskan Halibut with
Cantonese Lemon–Black Bean Sauce

○

Here's a second vibrantly flavored sauce that is delicious with halibut or other white-fleshed fish.

2 small dried black mushrooms

½ cup chicken stock

2 teaspoons oyster sauce

½ teaspoon salt

1½ teaspoons sugar

8 ounces halibut fillet

½ teaspoon sesame oil

2 tablespoons peanut or vegetable oil

2 tablespoons julienned scallion whites

1½ tablespoons julienned ginger

1 tablespoon julienned fresh
 red chile pepper

Zest of ½ lemon, julienned

1 teaspoon minced garlic

½ teaspoon Chinese salted
 black beans

1 tablespoon Shaoxing rice wine
 or dry sherry

¼ cup julienned scallion greens

A squeeze of lemon juice

Soak the mushrooms in hot water to cover for at least 30 minutes. When softened, cut off and discard the stems, and slice the caps into julienne; set aside.

Combine the chicken stock, oyster sauce, ½ teaspoon salt, and the sugar; set aside.

Rub the fish with the sesame oil and sprinkle with salt on both sides; set aside.

Heat a skillet or wok to very hot and add the peanut oil. When hot, add the fish. Sear briefly, then add the scallion whites, ginger, chile, lemon zest, garlic, black beans, and mushrooms, and sauté briefly. Add the stock mixture, cover, and cook over medium heat until the fish is just done, about 3 minutes (you may have to add a little more stock).

Remove the fish to a plate, leaving the sauce in the pan. Heat the sauce to boiling and add the Shaoxing wine. Sprinkle in the scallion greens and a squeeze of lemon and pour the sauce over the fish. Serve with steaming rice and seasonal vegetables.

Serves 2 as part of a larger meal

Teriyaki Ginger Salmon

○

This simple, teriyaki-style dish works well with a richer fish such as salmon, but will work with most any firm-fleshed fillet.

TERIYAKI SAUCE

1 tablespoon dark soy sauce

1 tablespoon light soy sauce

2½ tablespoons sugar

2 tablespoons peanut oil

8 ounces salmon fillet, preferably wild

2 tablespoons chopped ginger

1 tablespoon Shaoxing rice wine
   or dry sherry

2 tablespoons thinly sliced scallion

A small lemon wedge

Combine the soy sauces and sugar to make the teriyaki sauce, and set aside.

Heat the pan or skillet to very hot. Add the oil. Sear the fish in the pan skin side down. Turn and sear the other side. Add the ginger and sauté briefly. Add ¼ cup water and cover the pan. Steam for 2 to 3 minutes, adding more water as necessary. Uncover and add the teriyaki sauce, and, as the sauce reduces to a syrup, turn the fish in it a couple of times to glaze. When the sauce becomes a glaze, add the wine, scallion, and a squeeze of the lemon. Turn the fish once or twice more until well glazed and remove to a serving dish. Serve with rice and any vegetables you choose such as Stir-Fried Snow Peas with Dried Black Mushrooms (page 53).

Serves 2 as part of a larger meal

Alaskan Halibut
with Basil-Coconut Sauce

○

The light and delicious creaminess of this Southeast Asian coconut sauce is offset by the clean flavors of ginger, lemongrass, chile peppers, basil, and fresh lime juice. It's wonderful with any white-fleshed fish such as halibut, sea bass, or grouper.

4 ounces coconut milk

2 tablespoons chopped fresh ginger

1 tablespoon chopped lemongrass

8 ounces fresh halibut fillet

½ teaspoon sesame oil

Salt

⅓ cup chicken stock

1½ tablespoons fish sauce

1 teaspoon sugar

3 tablespoons peanut oil

¼ cup thinly sliced red onion

1 tablespoon julienned fresh fresno or other hot chile

Juice of ½ small lime

¼ cup julienned fresh Asian basil leaves

2 tablespoons packed cilantro leaves

Black pepper

In a stainless steel pot, cook the coconut milk down over medium-low heat until it reduces to about ¼ cup. The last minute or so of cooking add the ginger and lemongrass. This can be done ahead of time.

Sprinkle the fish with the sesame oil and salt, and set aside.

Mix the chicken stock with the fish sauce and sugar; set aside.

Heat a skillet or small wok to hot and add the peanut oil. When hot, add the fish and sear briefly over high heat. Add the red onion and fresno chile, and sauté briefly. Add the stock mixture, bring to a boil, and cover. Cook until just done, 3 or 4 minutes, and remove the fish to a serving plate, leaving the sauce in the pan.

Over medium heat, stir the seasoned and reduced coconut milk into the sauce in the pan. Cook until hot. Add the fresh lime juice, cook for 5 to 10 seconds, and stir in the basil and cilantro.

Pour the sauce over the fish. Sprinkle with pepper. Serve with steaming hot rice and seasonal vegetables such as Chinese Broccoli with Oyster Sauce (page 51).

Serves 2 as part of a larger meal

Wok-Seared and Steamed Halibut with Fresh Tomatoes

○

Best in the summer with red ripe tomatoes, this sauce is loaded with ginger, which has a wonderful affinity for tomatoes. It's seasoned as well with garlic, crisp fresh water chestnuts, and fresh cilantro leaves. The sauce is excellent with any flaky, white-fleshed fish such as halibut.

One 8- to 10-ounce halibut fillet
    or other firm-fleshed white fish

1 teaspoon sesame oil

1¼ teaspoons salt

¾ pound red ripe tomatoes,
    peeled and seeded

4½ tablespoons peanut oil

2 teaspoons sugar

2 tablespoons finely chopped ginger

1 tablespoon finely chopped garlic

4 fresh water chestnuts, sliced

½ cup chicken stock

½ cup fresh cilantro leaves

Rub the fish with the sesame oil and sprinkle with ½ teaspoon of the salt; set aside.

Cut the tomatoes into 1-inch cubes; set aside.

To make the fresh tomato sauce, heat a wok or skillet until nearly smoking. Add 1½ tablespoons of the peanut oil. When hot, add the tomatoes (watch the spattering) and cook, stirring, over high heat. Stir in the remaining ¾ teaspoon of salt and the sugar. Continue to cook over high heat for 2 or 3 minutes, until the tomatoes just start to soften and the sauce thickens slightly. Remove to a bowl, stir in another 2 teaspoons of the oil, and set aside.

Heat a skillet to hot; add 2 tablespoons peanut oil. When hot, add the fish and sear briefly. Add the ginger and garlic next to the fish and stir briefly to release their flavor. Add the water chestnuts and stir briefly; then add the chicken stock and cover. Turn the heat to medium and steam for 3 minutes or until the fish is done to your liking.

Remove the fish to a serving plate with a slotted spoon; add the reserved tomato sauce to the pan, and turn up the heat on the sauce. Cook just until it reaches the desired consistency, about 20 seconds. Turn off the heat, stir in the cilantro leaves, pour over the fish, and serve with rice.

Serves 2 as part of a larger meal

Shanghai Shrimp
with Shiitake and Rice Wine

○

This classic, almost buttery combination typifies the cooking of Eastern China at its most refined. The seasonings include bamboo shoots, ginger, scallion, shiitake, and Shaoxing rice wine. This is an elegant shrimp dish.

2 large dried mushrooms

½ pound shrimp, peeled and
    cut in half lengthwise

2 teaspoons cornstarch

1 teaspoon sesame oil plus
    a few drops for garnish

SAUCE

¼ cup chicken stock

1 tablespoon light soy sauce

¼ teaspoon kosher salt

1 teaspoon sugar

1 cup peanut oil

¼ cup julienned bamboo shoots

2 tablespoons julienned ginger

2 tablespoons Shaoxing rice wine

¼ cup sliced scallion greens

½ cup fresh cilantro leaves

1 teaspoon freshly ground
    white pepper

Soak the mushrooms for 30 minutes in hot water to cover. When soft, cut off and discard the stems, and slice the mushrooms thinly. Mix the shrimp with the cornstarch and 1 teaspoon sesame oil.

To make the sauce, combine the chicken stock, soy sauce, salt, and sugar; set aside.

Heat 1 cup oil in a wok or skillet. When hot but not smoking, add the shrimp. Cook, stirring, to separate the pieces. When the shrimp change color, immediately remove and drain in a colander. Reserve the oil.

Heat a clean wok or skillet to hot and add ¼ cup of the reserved oil. When very hot, add the mushroom slices, bamboo shoots, and ginger, and cook, stirring, for about 1 minute over high heat. Add the chicken stock mixture and bring to a boil. Add the shrimp and cook, stirring to coat the shrimp with the sauce and seasonings. When piping hot, add the wine and scallion. Stir then turn off the heat. Stir in the cilantro leaves and white pepper. Drizzle with the sesame oil. Serve with rice.

Serves 2 to 3 as part of a larger meal

Shrimp and Chicken
with Thai Basil and Red Onion

○

This combination of shrimp—both fresh and dried—and chicken, is loaded with sweet red onion and basil, and has irresistible flavor.

4 ounces boneless chicken breast, sliced

2 teaspoons cornstarch

1 teaspoon sesame oil

½ teaspoon salt

4 ounces shrimp, peeled, deveined, and cut in half lengthwise

3 tablespoons fish sauce

2½ tablespoons freshly squeezed lime juice

5 teaspoons sugar

1 cup peanut oil

1 cup cut-up red onions (cut into 1-inch square pieces)

1 tablespoon fresh ginger

1 teaspoon fresh garlic

1 teaspoon finely minced lemongrass

¼ cup tightly packed Thai basil leaves

1 tablespoon chopped roasted peanuts

2 teaspoons ground dried shrimp

Fresh cilantro leaves for garnish

Put the chicken breast in a small bowl and mix with 1 teaspoon of the cornstarch, ½ teaspoon of the sesame oil, and the ½ teaspoon salt. Add the shrimp to the bowl. Mix in the remaining cornstarch and sesame oil. Set aside.

Combine the fish sauce, lime juice, and sugar.

In a wok or skillet, heat 1 cup peanut oil over medium-high heat. When hot but not smoking, add the chicken and shrimp, and cook, stirring to separate the pieces. When the pieces change color, remove to a colander to drain, reserving the oil.

Heat a clean wok or skillet to hot and add ¼ cup of the reserved oil. Add the onions and cook, stirring until they just become transparent. Add the ginger, garlic, and lemongrass, and stir briefly. Turn the heat to high and re-add the chicken and shrimp. Stir and add the fish sauce mixture. Bring just to a boil, stir in the basil, and remove from the heat. Stir in the peanuts and dried shrimp. Garnish with the cilantro and serve with rice.

Serves 2 to 3 as part of a larger meal

Shrimp with Cantonese Black Beans, Scallions, and Ginger

○

There are three reasons why many think the Cantonese serve some of the best seafood on earth. One, it's fresh, which means when ordered, it's scooped from a tank. Two, it's expertly cooked, until just done. Three, it's delicately seasoned, often with the combination of salted black beans, ginger, and scallions below. This is a simple dish.

½ pound fresh shrimp, peeled and deveined

3 teaspoons cornstarch

1½ teaspoons sesame oil

⅓ cup chicken stock

1 teaspoon oyster sauce

1 teaspoon salt

1 teaspoon sugar

1 cup peanut oil

½ cup julienned scallions

2 tablespoons finely julienned ginger

2 teaspoons minced garlic

1 rounded teaspoon Chinese black beans, rubbed together between one's hands

2 tablespoons Shaoxing rice wine or dry sherry

½ teaspoon fresh ground white pepper

Cilantro sprigs for garnish

Cut the shrimp in half lengthwise and mix with 2 teaspoons cornstarch and 1 teaspoon sesame oil; set aside. Allow to sit for 15 minutes or more. Mix the remaining teaspoon of cornstarch with 1 tablespoon of water and set aside.

Combine the chicken stock, oyster sauce, salt, and sugar; set aside.

In a wok or skillet, heat 1 cup peanut oil to hot but not smoking. When the oil is hot, add the shrimp and cook, stirring, just until the shrimp changes color. Remove to drain in a colander. Drain and reserve the oil.

Heat a clean wok or skillet to very hot and add 3 tablespoons of the reserved oil. When hot, add the scallions, ginger, garlic, and black beans and cook, stirring rapidly for about 20 seconds. Add the chicken stock mixture and bring to a boil. Re-stir the cornstarch-water mixture and add it. When the sauce thickens slightly and clears, re-add the shrimp. Cook, stirring briefly, and add the wine. Give it a toss and sprinkle with the remaining sesame oil and the white pepper. Garnish with cilantro sprigs and serve with rice.

Serves 2 to 3 as part of a larger meal

Shrimp with Peas, Tree Ear Mushrooms, and Barbecued Pork

○

This is a colorful shrimp dish full of pleasing textures including fresh water chestnuts. The barbecued pork here, rather than a feature, is more of a highlight, sprinkled throughout, that seasons the dish.

8–10 small dried tree ear mushrooms (flake-like pieces no more than ½ inch in length)

½ pound shrimp, peeled and cut in half lengthwise

2 teaspoons cornstarch

Sesame oil

SAUCE

½ cup chicken stock

1 tablespoons oyster sauce

1 teaspoon light soy sauce

½ teaspoon kosher salt

2 teaspoons sugar

1 cup peanut oil

1 tablespoon chopped ginger

⅓ cup Chinese Barbecued Pork Shoulder (page 23) cut into ¼-inch dice

¼ cup fresh water chestnuts, peeled and sliced

½ cup frozen peas (or fresh peas that have been parboiled)

2 teaspoons cornstarch mixed with 2 tablespoons of water

2 tablespoons Shaoxing rice wine

¼ cup sliced scallion greens

¼ cup fresh cilantro leaves

Soak the mushrooms for 30 minutes in hot water to cover. When soft, drain and set aside.

Mix the shrimp with 2 teaspoons cornstarch and 1 teaspoon sesame oil. Mix the remaining 2 teaspoons of cornstarch with 3 tablespoons of water and set aside.

Combine the chicken stock, soy sauce, salt, and sugar; set aside.

Heat 1 cup of peanut oil in a wok or skillet. When the oil is hot but not smoking, add the shrimp. Cook stirring to separate the pieces. When the shrimp change color, immediately remove and drain in a colander. Reserve the oil.

Heat a clean wok or skillet over high heat and add ¼ cup of the reserved oil. When the oil is very hot, add the tree ear mushrooms, ginger, and barbecued pork, and cook stirring briefly. Add the water chestnuts and peas and continue to cook.

Add the chicken stock mixture and bring to a boil. Re-add the shrimp and cook, stirring to coat the shrimp, with the sauce and seasonings. Give the cornstarch and water mixture a stir to recombine it and add to the pan. When piping hot, add the wine and the scallions. Stir, then turn off the heat. Stir in the coriander leaves, drizzle with the sesame oil. Serve with rice.

Serves 2 to 3 as part of a larger meal

Shrimp with Fresh-Shucked Corn and Sugar Snap Peas

○

A late summer dish, this works best when the corn is local, is very sweet, and is shucked at the last minute.

2 to 3 ears fresh sweet corn

10 sugar snap peas

¾ cup chicken stock

2 teaspoons oyster sauce

2 teaspoons light soy sauce

1½ teaspoons sugar

2¼ teaspoons kosher salt

½ pound shrimp, freshly peeled and deveined

4 teaspoons cornstarch

1½ teaspoons sesame oil

1 cup peanut or vegetable oil

3 to 4 fresh shiitake or oyster mushrooms or other fresh mushrooms, sliced

¼ cup thinly sliced scallion whites

1 fresh red chile pepper, minced, seeds and all

2 teaspoons chopped garlic

2 tablespoons Shaoxing rice wine or dry sherry

1 teaspoon freshly ground black pepper

Husk and, with a knife, cut the corn kernels off the cob into a mixing bowl. Cut the strings off the snap peas, and set aside.

Combine the chicken stock, oyster sauce, light soy sauce, sugar, and 2 teaspoons of the salt; set aside.

Cut the shrimp in half lengthwise and toss the halves with 2 teaspoons of the cornstarch, the remaining ¼ teaspoon salt, and 1 teaspoon of the sesame oil. Mix the remaining 2 teaspoons of cornstarch with 2 tablespoons of water; set aside.

Heat 1 cup peanut oil in a wok or skillet until hot but not smoking. When hot, add the shrimp and stir, separating the pieces, just until the shrimp changes color. Remove from the oil with a slotted spoon to drain. Remove the oil from the pan and reserve.

Reheat the pan over high heat. When hot, add 4 to 5 tablespoons of the reserved peanut oil. When hot, add the mushrooms and stir for 15 seconds or so, then add the scallion and chile pepper. Cook, stirring, for 1 minute, until the mushrooms are softened. Add the garlic and stir briefly, then add the corn and snap peas, and cook, stirring, over high heat for 1 minute. Add the stock mixture, bring to a boil, turn the heat to medium, and simmer until the corn is cooked, 2 minutes or so; re-add the shrimp.

Turn the heat to high. Re-stir the cornstarch-water mixture and add. Stir over high heat until the sauce thickens and clears. Splash in the wine and continue to stir briefly. Spoon into a serving bowl or platter and serve sprinkled with the remaining sesame oil and the black pepper, and accompanied by white rice.

Serves 2 as a complete meal, 4 as part of larger meal

Singapore Chili Shrimp

○

Singapore Chili Crab, known to anyone who eats in Singapore, has an egg and tomato–based sauce that is loaded with ginger and garlic. Here's a version with shrimp.

1 pound shrimp, unpeeled

2 teaspoons light soy sauce

1 teaspoon chili paste with garlic

1 tablespoon sugar

½ teaspoon salt

5 tablespoons peanut oil

1 cup drained and lightly chopped
    canned tomatoes

2 tablespoons ginger, finely chopped

1 tablespoon garlic, finely chopped

1 large egg, lightly beaten

½ cup lightly chopped cilantro leaves

Few drops sesame oil for garnish

Peel the shrimp, leaving on the tail section. Devein.

Combine the soy sauce, chili paste with garlic, sugar, and salt; set aside.

Heat a skillet over high heat and when smoking hot, add 2 tablespoons of the oil. Add the tomatoes (watch out for the spattering) and cook, stirring, over high heat, about 1 to 2 minutes, until they thicken slightly. Add the soy sauce mixture and continue to cook another minute or so; set aside.

Heat another wok or skillet to hot. When hot, add the remaining 3 tablespoons of oil. When the oil is hot, add the ginger and garlic, and toss briefly. Add the shrimp and stir until they are well coated with the seasonings and start to turn color. Then add the tomato sauce and cook over high heat until piping hot. Turn off the heat; immediately stir in the egg, sprinkle in the cilantro, drizzle with the sesame oil, and serve accompanied by rice.

Serves 3 to 4 as part of a large meal

Burmese Shrimp and Chicken Curry

○

A mild, lightly creamy fresh curry that combines shrimp, chicken breast, and fresh snap peas. It's also wonderfully colorful.

⅔ cup canned unsweetened
    coconut milk

5 large shrimp, peeled and deveined,
    tail section intact

4 ounces chicken breast, sliced

2 teaspoons cornstarch

1 teaspoon sesame oil

2 teaspoons fish sauce

1 teaspoon fresh lime juice

1 teaspoon sugar

1 cup peanut or vegetable oil

2 tablespoons julienned fresh
    red hot or sweet peppers

12 sugar snap peas

2 heaping tablespoons fresh curry
    paste (pages 16 and 17)

¼ cup chicken stock

Put the coconut milk in a saucepan and, over medium heat, reduce to about ½ cup. Set aside. Toss the shrimp and chicken with the cornstarch and sesame oil, and set aside.

Combine the fish sauce, lime juice, and sugar.

Warm a small wok or saucepan over high heat and add 1 cup oil. When hot but not smoking, add the shrimp and chicken, and cook, stirring, just until they turn translucent. Remove to drain; reserve the oil.

Heat a clean wok or skillet over high heat and add 2 teaspoons of the reserved oil. Add the peppers and snap peas, and stir until well coated with the oil. Push the vegetables slightly to the side and add the curry paste to the pan. Cook briefly, stirring, and add the chicken stock. When it boils, add the reduced coconut milk. When hot, stir in the shrimp and chicken. Add the fish sauce-sugar-lime juice mixture. Stir just to heat and serve with or over rice.

Serves 2 with rice as a complete meal, 4 as part of a larger meal

Sea Scallops with Tomatoes and Fresh Water Chestnuts

○

There's a highly refined sense of texture in Chinese cooking. Here two ingredients, nearly identical in shape and color—scallops and fresh water chestnuts— are paired for the delight provided by their contrasting textures. There's the yin of the cool crisp water chestnut versus the yang of the rich soft bite of the scallop.

½ pound sea scallops, cut in half (semicircles)

1 teaspoon cornstarch

1¼ teaspoons salt

1 teaspoon sesame oil

1½ pounds red ripe tomatoes, peeled and seeded

1 cup plus 5 tablespoons peanut oil

1 tablespoon sugar

2 tablespoons finely chopped ginger

1 tablespoon finely chopped garlic

⅓ cup fresh water chestnuts, peeled and cut in half like the scallops

8 fresh sugar snap peas

Mix the scallops with the cornstarch, ¼ teaspoon of the salt, and the sesame oil, and set aside. Cut the tomatoes into quarters if small; if large cut them into eighths.

Heat a wok or skillet over high heat until nearly smoking. Add 2 tablespoons of the peanut oil. When hot, add the tomatoes (watch out for the spattering). Stir and add the remaining 1 teaspoon of salt and the sugar. Cook over high heat for 3 or 4 minutes, until the tomatoes just start to soften and the sauce thickens slightly. Remove to a bowl, stir in another tablespoon of oil, and set aside.

Heat 1 cup peanut oil in a wok or skillet until hot but not smoking. Add the scallops and cook, stirring, just until they turn opaque. Remove the scallops to a colander to drain and reserve the oil.

Heat a clean wok or skillet over high heat. When hot, add 2 tablespoons of peanut oil. When the oil is hot, add the ginger and garlic, and stir briefly. Add the fresh water chestnuts and snap peas, and continue to stir for about 20 seconds.

Pour in the reserved tomato sauce. When combined and boiling, add the scallops; stir just to heat and serve with rice.

Serves 2 as a compete meal, 3 to 4 as part of a larger meal

Hot and Sour Sea Scallops
with Blackened Chile Peppers

○

An authentic hot vinegar sauce from Western China that we serve with various seafood combinations—here to delicious effect with sea scallops.

2 small dried black mushrooms

8 ounces fresh sea scallops, cut in half (like half moons)

1 tablespoon cornstarch

1 teaspoon sesame oil plus a few drops for sprinkling

4 freshly peeled fresh water chestnuts

2 tablespoons red wine vinegar

2 tablespoons rice vinegar

7 teaspoons light soy sauce

2 tablespoons sugar

1 cup peanut oil

5 to 6 dried chiles

2 tablespoon finely chopped fresh ginger

1 tablespoon finely chopped fresh garlic

¼ cup finely sliced scallions (whites only)

¼ cup finely sliced scallion greens

Few sprigs cilantro for garnish

Soak the mushrooms in hot water to cover for at least 30 minutes. When softened, cut off and discard the stems, slice the caps in thirds, and set aside.

Marinate the scallops in the cornstarch and the 1 teaspoon sesame oil and set aside. Cut the water chestnuts like the scallops.

Combine the vinegars, light soy sauce, and sugar, and stir until the sugar dissolves.

Heat a small skillet or wok over medium-high heat and add the peanut oil. When hot add the scallops and cook, stirring, until just opaque. Remove and drain. Reserve the oil.

Heat a clean wok or skillet to hot and add ¼ cup of the reserved oil. Add the chile peppers and cook over medium-high heat until the peppers blacken and smoke. Add the mushrooms and stir briefly. Add the water chestnuts, ginger, garlic, and scallion whites, and cook briefly, stirring or tossing. Re-add the scallops and cook briefly, tossing until they're coated with the herbs. (Don't allow the ginger or garlic to brown.) Turn the heat to high, add the vinegar mixture, and bring to a boil. Just when it comes to a rapid boil, remove from the heat, sprinkle in the scallion greens, and transfer to a serving plate. Sprinkle with the sesame oil, garnish with the cilantro, and serve with white rice.

Serves 3 to 4 as part of a larger meal

Scallops with Oyster Mushrooms, Peas, and Snow Peas

○

This is a simple and elegant stir-fry that combines fresh sea scallops and oyster mushrooms, a mushroom cultivated in Asia for centuries that tastes vaguely of the sea, hence its name. Oyster mushrooms are available all year in Asian groceries and, increasingly, in many supermarkets.

SAUCE

½ cup chicken stock

2 teaspoons oyster sauce

2 teaspoons Chinese light soy sauce

1 teaspoon salt

1½ teaspoons sugar

8 ounces fresh sea scallops, each cut into 2 semicircles

2 teaspoons cornstarch

Sesame oil

Peanut or vegetable oil

⅓ cup fresh oyster mushrooms, cut in half across the cap

1 tablespoon finely chopped ginger

1 teaspoon finely chopped garlic

4 fresh water chestnuts, peeled and cut in half (like the scallops)

12–15 snow peas (or sugar snap peas), strung

¼ cup fresh or frozen peas

2 teaspoons cornstarch blended with 2 tablespoons water

1 tablespoon Shaoxing rice wine or dry sherry

Mix the sauce by combining the chicken stock with the oyster sauce, soy sauce, salt, and sugar.

Mix the scallops with the cornstarch and ½ teaspoon sesame oil.

Heat 1 cup peanut oil in a wok or skillet until hot but not smoking. When the oil is hot add the scallops and stir, separating the pieces, just until the they change color, and remove from the oil with a slotted spoon to drain.

Remove all the oil from the wok or skillet, reserve it, wipe the pan, and reheat over high heat. When the oil is hot, add 4 tablespoons of the reserved peanut oil. Add the mushrooms and cook, stirring, for 30 seconds, then add the ginger, garlic, and water chestnuts and stir briefly. Add the snow peas and peas and stir for another 30 seconds.

Add the chicken stock mixture and bring to a boil; return the scallops and cook briefly. Stir the cornstarch-water mixture to recombine it and add. Stir until the sauce thickens and clears. Put on a plate and serve sprinkled with a little sesame oil and accompanied by steaming white rice.

Serves 2 as a main course, 3 to 4 as part of a larger meal

Crunchy Sichuan Sesame Shrimp

○

One of the few golden-fried items in the Big Bowl repertoire, this "crunchy" shrimp dish, developed by my colleague Matt McMillin, has a light but very fiery glaze to it, and the great complementary flavors of chile peppers and bamboo shoots, the yang and yin of Sichuan cooking, predominates. It's best eaten immediately after it's prepared.

¾ pound fresh shrimp, peeled and deveined

BATTER

2 teaspoons sesame oil

I egg white, lightly beaten

I tablespoon cornstarch

2 tablespoons flour

2 tablespoons Japanese bread crumbs (panko)

I tablespoon sesame seeds

SAUCE

2 teaspoons red wine vinegar

¼ teaspoon dark soy sauce

2 teaspoons light soy sauce

2 teaspoons sugar

2 tablespoons hoisin sauce

I tablespoon bean sauce

2 teaspoons chili paste with garlic

Peanut oil

½ cup julienned bamboo shoots

¼ cup julienned fresh red chile pepper

I tablespoon minced fresh garlic

⅓ cup scallion whites, cut into I-inch lengths

¼ cup chicken stock

½ teaspoon cornstarch mixed with 2 teaspoons water

¼ cup cilantro leaves

Few drops sesame oil

Cut the shrimp in half lengthwise and mix with the sesame oil and egg white. Combine the rest of the batter ingredients and mix with the shrimp by hand, making sure they are well coated with the batter.

Combine the sauce ingredients.

Heat 4 to 6 cups of oil in a wok or skillet to 375 degrees. Cook the shrimp in two batches, each for 30 seconds and remove with a slotted spoon to drain on paper towels. Maintain the oil at 375 degrees while you make the sauce. (You will fry the shrimp briefly again.)

Heat a small skillet or wok over high heat and add 3 tablespoons of oil. Add the bamboo shoots, chile pepper, ginger, and scallion whites; cook, stirring, for 20 seconds. Add the sauce mixture and, when it's boiling hot, add the stock. When the mixture boils, give the cornstarch-water mixture a quick stir to recombine, and add it. When the sauce is hot and clear and has a slight glaze, remove the pan from the heat.

Reheat the frying oil if necessary to 375–400 degrees and add all the shrimp. Fry briefly and remove to drain. When well drained, add the shrimp to the sauce and toss to glaze the shrimp. Toss in the cilantro leaves, sprinkle with the sesame oil, and serve with plain rice.

Serves 2 as a main course, 3 to 4 as part of a larger meal

13 MEAT

Stir-Fried Hunan Pork Loin with Fresh Chiles and Bamboo Shoots

○

This simple stir-fried dish combines the fire of fresh chiles with the cooling texture of bamboo shoots, all in a simple wine sauce. It is one of the most easily prepared dishes in the book.

3 large dried black mushrooms

WINE SAUCE

¼ cup Shaoxing rice wine

2 teaspoons sugar

1½ teaspoons kosher salt

8 ounces pork loin (the meat from a couple of pork chops), cut into julienned strips

2 teaspoons dark soy sauce

2 teaspoons sesame oil

4 tablespoons peanut oil

½ cup julienned fresh red chiles

⅓ cup julienned bamboo shoots

Soak the mushrooms in hot water to cover for 30 minutes. Then squeeze out some of the moisture and thinly slice.

To make the wine sauce, combine the Shaoxing wine, sugar, and salt; set aside.

Toss the pork shreds with the dark soy sauce and sesame oil, and set aside.

Heat a wok or skillet over high heat to nearly smoking. Add the peanut oil. When hot, add the pork and stir briefly just until the shreds separate and change color. Add the mushroom slices.

Stir briefly, then add the chiles and bamboo shoots and cook, stirring, until the vegetables soften slightly, 1 to 2 minutes. The pan should be piping hot. Add the wine sauce (it should sizzle) and continue to stir and toss another 15 to 30 seconds. Serve with white rice.

Serves 2 with rice as a complete meal, 3 to 4 as part of a larger meal

Sichuan-Style Bean Curd
(Ma Po Doufu)

○

Since the 1960s, when this dish was first introduced to American palates via the first Sichuan restaurants, this home-style dish, loaded with garlic, ginger, and hot bean sauce, has become a menu staple of U.S. Sichuan restaurants. This is a classic version that explodes with flavor.

1 tablespoon Sichuan peppercorns

1 pound fresh firm bean curd

1 cup ground pork (about 6 ounces)

2 teaspoons dark soy sauce

3 tablespoons peanut or vegetable oil

1 tablespoon (or more) chopped fresh chile peppers

1 tablespoon chopped garlic

1 tablespoon chopped fresh ginger

3 tablespoons Chinese whole bean sauce

2 teaspoons sugar

¾ cup chicken stock

2 teaspoons cornstarch mixed with 2 tablespoons water

½ cup finely sliced scallion greens

1 teaspoon sesame oil

A few cilantro sprigs for garnish

Warm a small skillet over medium heat and add the peppercorns. Toast, shaking the skillet, until the peppercorns begin to smoke. Transfer to a spice grinder and grind to a coarse powder. Set aside 1 teaspoon of the powder.

Cut the bean curd into ¾-inch cubes and set aside.

Mix the pork with the dark soy sauce and set aside.

Warm a large skillet or wok over high heat and add the oil. Add the chiles, garlic, and ginger; stir briefly. Add the pork and stir to separate the pieces, taking care not to brown. Sprinkle in the Sichuan peppercorn powder and continue to stir. After the pork is hot and has changed color, add the bean sauce and sugar, and stir until combined.

Add the bean curd and cook, stirring, until the mixture is hot, about 1 minute. Add the stock and bring to a boil. Cook another minute.

When the mixture is boiling hot, give the cornstarch dish a quick stir to combine and add. Cook, stirring, until hot and shiny. Turn off the heat and toss in the scallions. Serve dribbled with the sesame oil and garnished with the cilantro and accompanied by steaming hot rice.

Serves 3 to 4 as part of a larger meal

Braised Baby Spareribs
with Black Beans and Garlic

Unlike most of the recipes in this book which call for quick cooking, this wintry dish is slowly braised until the ribs are meltingly tender; it's delicious reheated.

2½ pounds pork spareribs, cut across the bones into 3 strips (see Note)

¼ cup peanut oil

½ cup diced yellow onion

2 tablespoons chopped garlic

2 tablespoons chopped ginger

1 tablespoon salted black beans, lightly mashed with the back of a spoon

½ cup Shaoxing rice wine

1 tablespoon dark soy sauce

2 teaspoons sugar

1½ teaspoons kosher salt

½ cup fresh cilantro leaves

Cut the ribs into individual pieces, rinse and dry.

Warm a wok, a large skillet, or a heavy pot over high heat and add the oil. When hot, add the onion and cook until translucent. Add the garlic, ginger, and black beans, and cook for another 30 seconds. Add the ribs and cook, stirring, for 1 to 2 minutes until the ribs are well coated with the seasonings. Add the wine and when it boils, pour over the mixture 2 cups hot water. Add the dark soy sauce, sugar, and salt, and bring to a boil. Turn the heat to low, cover, and simmer, checking from time to time, for 45 minutes to an hour. You may have to add more water. When the ribs are tender, just before they fall off the bone, remove them from the sauce and cover. Turn the heat up to high and reduce the sauce until it thickens slightly but doesn't separate. It should be thick enough to coat the ribs. Re-add the ribs and cook, stirring briefly. Turn off the heat, stir in the cilantro leaves, and serve with hot white rice.

NOTE: Ask the butcher cut the rack across the bone into three sections so the ribs are 1½ to 2 inches long.

Serves 3 to 4 as part of a larger meal

Beef with Thai Basil

○

Lightly creamy and loaded with fragrant basil, this beef dish goes well with rice, or it can be stir-fried with Chinese egg noodles or Pad Thai rice noodles.

⅔ cup coconut milk

1 tablespoon minced ginger

1½ tablespoons fish sauce

¾ pound flank steak, thinly sliced across the grain

2 teaspoons dark soy sauce

2 teaspoons cornstarch

1 teaspoon sesame oil

2 cups peanut oil

½ cup finely sliced red onion

¼ cup julienned fresh red chile pepper

⅓ cup chicken stock

½ teaspoon salt

½ teaspoon sugar

½ cup tightly packed Thai basil leaves

Juice of ¼ large lime

½ teaspoon freshly ground black pepper for garnish

Cilantro leaves for garnish

Simmer the coconut milk in a stainless steel pan for 5 minutes. Add the ginger and continue simmering until it reduces to ½ cup. Stir in the fish sauce and turn off the heat.

Marinate the beef in the dark soy sauce, cornstarch, and the sesame oil for 30 minutes.

Heat 2 cups peanut oil in a pot or wok until hot but not smoking. Add the beef and cook, separating the slices, until the meat starts to change color but remains rare. Remove and drain, reserving the oil.

Heat a clean wok or skillet to hot, add 3 tablespoons of the reserved oil, and when hot, add the red onion and chile, and stir until the onion turns translucent. Add the coconut milk and chicken stock, sprinkle in the salt and sugar, and bring to a simmer. Add the beef and cook, stirring, briefly. Add the basil, toss, and then add the fresh lime juice. Toss again and serve garnished with the pepper and fresh cilantro.

Serves 3 to 4 as part of a larger meal

Orange Peel Beef

○

A Chinese-American classic whose history goes back to at least the 1960s in New York City, where sweet and sour was updated with citrus and spices at newly opened "Hunan" restaurants. Our version uses freshly squeezed lemon juice and orange slices.

¾ pound flank steak, cut into
    1 x 2-inch slices

2 teaspoons dark soy sauce

1 egg, beaten

¼ cup flour

2 tablespoons cornstarch

½ teaspoon salt

ORANGE SAUCE

2 tablespoons light soy sauce

¼ cup lemon juice

5 ½ tablespoons sugar

¼ teaspoon salt

3 tablespoons julienned scallion

3 tablespoons julienned ginger

8 slices red chile pepper, julienned

2 fresh water chestnuts, peeled
    and sliced

2¼ cups peanut oil

3 thin orange slices, peeled
    and cut into quarters

¼ cup chicken stock

1 tablespoon cornstarch mixed
    with ¼ cup water

Rub the beef slices with the dark soy sauce. Then mix the slices with the beaten egg, flour, cornstarch, and salt. Let sit for 10 minutes and, rubbing with your fingers, work the beef together with the flour mixture again—repeat in another 10 minutes.

Meanwhile, make the orange sauce. Combine the light soy sauce, lemon juice, sugar, and salt.

In a bowl put the scallion, ginger, chile pepper shreds, and fresh water chestnuts.

In a wok or skillet, heat 2 cups of the peanut oil to 375 degrees. Keep it at that temperature while you cook the sauce.

Heat a skillet or saucepan to hot and add the remaining ¼ cup peanut oil. When hot, add the scallion-ginger mixture. Cook, stirring rapidly, for about 15 seconds just to coat with the oil. Add the orange slices and cook another 10 seconds. Add the orange sauce and chicken stock, and bring to a boil. Recombine the cornstarch-water mixture and add to the sauce. Allow to boil, thicken, and clear, then turn off the heat.

Meanwhile, add the beef to the oil and fry until crispy. Remove to drain. Then immediately add the meat to the sauce you just made and toss briefly to coat. Serve with rice.

Serves 4 as part of a larger meal

Red Braised Beef Short Ribs

○

A specialty of Shanghai, "red braising" refers to the slow simmering of rich meats in Shaoxing rice wine, Chinese rock sugar, and dark soy sauce. Usually pork shoulder, fresh bacon, duck, or, as in this case, beef short ribs. Here the beef is complemented by the Asian radish known by its Japanese name, "daikon," which is often served with rich dishes as it is a great foil for a delicious sauce and is thought to help in the digestion of rich foods.

A variation of this dish, served over noodles, is offered on page 147.

3 pounds beef short ribs, cut in half across the ribs by your butcher

½ cup Shaoxing rice wine

3 whole star anise

2 teaspoons dark soy sauce

¼ cup light soy sauce

1 large lump of yellow rock sugar (roughly 1½ inches square)

½ teaspoon kosher salt

½ pound daikon (Asian white radish) cut into 1-inch pieces

½ cup fresh cilantro leaves

Place the ribs in a pot with 1 quart water and bring to a boil. Skim well and add the Shaoxing wine. Continue to skim if necessary and add the star anise. Turn the heat to medium-low and simmer for 10 minutes.

Add the soy sauces, rock sugar, and salt, and simmer, covered, over low heat for an hour. Add the daikon and cook for another 45 minutes. If necessary keep cooking until the meat is nearly ready to come off the bone. When cooked, remove the short ribs with a slotted spoon, and cover to keep warm.

Turn the heat to high under the sauce and reduce, uncovered, until it thickens slightly. Re-add the meat and cook briefly in the sauce (it should coat the meat). Stir in the cilantro leaves, remove to a platter, and serve with rice.

Serves 4 to 6 as part of a larger meal

Braised Short Ribs with Noodles

○

Braised short ribs are delicious when mixed with noodles. You can use leftover meat and sauce or you can start from scratch.

Using the recipe on page 146, once the meat is starting to fall off of the bone, remove it with a slotted spoon, leaving the sauce in the pot. When cool enough to handle, remove the meat from the bones and discard them. Break the meat up with your fingers as best you can. Meanwhile, reduce the sauce as described above. When the sauce is reduced to about ¾ cup, add the meat shreds and cook, stirring over low heat.

While the sauce is reducing—using either a pound of Shanghai noodles that have been precooked, drained, and oiled, or Pad Thai noodles that have been soaked and softened—put the noodles in a strainer, dip briefly in boiling water (when using the Pad Thai noodles be careful that they don't overcook), and arrange in a serving bowl. Add the fresh cilantro leaves to the meat. Immediately pour the meat and sauce over the noodles and serve.

You can also make this with any leftover braised ribs and sauce from the previous recipe—just cook correspondingly fewer noodles. The proportion should be slightly more cooked noodles in volume than you have leftover meat and sauce.

Starting from scratch, the recipe will serve 4 to 6 as part of a larger meal

Mongolian Lamb with Scallions

○

A fine (and simple) version of a popular Northern Chinese menu item.

SAUCE

2 teaspoons light soy sauce

1 teaspoon bean sauce

2 teaspoons hoisin sauce

2 teaspoons oyster sauce

1 teaspoon chili paste with garlic

2 teaspoons sugar

2 teaspoons red wine vinegar

¾ pound lamb loin, thinly sliced

2 teaspoons dark soy sauce

3 teaspoons cornstarch

1¼ teaspoons sesame oil

1½ cups peanut oil

4 fresh shiitake mushrooms or other fresh or wild mushrooms, sliced

¼ cup finely julienned ginger

6 garlic cloves, smashed

1½ cups thin scallions, cut into 2-inch lengths

⅓ cup chicken stock

1 tablespoon Shaoxing rice wine or dry sherry

Combine the sauce ingredients; set aside.

Marinate the lamb slices with the dark soy sauce, 2 teaspoons of the cornstarch, and 1 teaspoon of the sesame oil, and set aside. Mix the remaining teaspoon of cornstarch with 2 tablespoons water and place conveniently aside.

Heat 1½ cups oil in a wok or skillet. When hot but not smoking, add the lamb slices and cook, stirring, just to separate. While starting to change color, but still pink, remove them to a colander to drain. Reserve the oil.

Heat a wok or skillet over high heat and add 4 tablespoons of the reserved oil. When hot, add the mushrooms and sauté until wilted. Add the ginger and garlic and stir briefly; add the scallions and toss for 1 minute. Push the vegetables aside and pour in the sauce. Stir until it's boiling hot, then add the chicken stock. When hot, re-add the lamb, toss, then give the reserved cornstarch and water another stir and add it. Allow to boil and clear while you stir. Add the Shaoxing wine, give it a toss, drizzle with the remaining ¼ teaspoon sesame oil, and serve.

Serves 3 to 4 with rice as part of a larger meal

14 VEGETABLES

Eight Vegetable Stir-Fry

○

We use the number eight here because the Chinese regard it as lucky. This may be made with almost any combination of fresh vegetables using the technique and sauce combination below.

4 dried black mushrooms (shiitake)

¼ pound fresh green beans

6 snow peas or snap peas

¼ pound small bok choy leaves

¼ cup sliced bamboo shoots

2 scallions, cut into 2-inch lengths

½ cup chicken stock

3 tablespoons oyster sauce

½ teaspoon salt

½ teaspoon sugar

2 teaspoons cornstarch

¼ cup peanut or vegetable oil

1 teaspoon minced garlic

½ pound bean curd, cut into ¾ inch cubes

A few drops sesame oil

Cover the mushrooms with ½ cup boiling water and allow to sit for 30 minutes or longer.

Meanwhile, wash and prepare all the vegetables and set aside on a platter.

Combine the stock with the oyster sauce, salt, and sugar, and set aside.

Drain the mushrooms, reserving the liquid. Cut off the stems and discard; cut each cap in two.

Mix 4 tablespoons of the reserved liquid with the cornstarch and set aside.

Heat a large skillet or wok over high heat and add the peanut oil. Add the mushroom caps and garlic, and stir briefly. Add all the vegetables and stir rapidly until well coated with the oil, about 1 minute. Add the bean curd and continue to stir.

Add the chicken stock mixture and when it boils, give the cornstarch mixture a quick stir and add it. Cook, stirring, over high heat until the sauce gives a clear glaze to the vegetables. Serve sprinkled with the sesame oil.

Serves 1 or 3 with rice as a complete meal, 3 to 4 as part of a larger meal

Big Buddha Bowl

○

This is simply a large bowl of steamed vegetables over rice, served with a sauce on the side. It's vegetarian and doesn't use oil. The vegetables total slightly over a pound in weight.

3 dried black mushrooms

BIG BUDDHA
VEGETABLE SAUCE

¾ cup vegetarian broth (page 66)

1 tablespoon vegetable oyster sauce (available at Chinese markets)

½ teaspoon sugar

1 teaspoon chopped garlic

1 teaspoon chopped ginger

2 teaspoons cornstarch mixed with 2 tablespoons vegetarian broth or water

⅓ cup bean curd, cubed

6 snow peas

¼ cup bamboo shoots, sliced

4 hearts of Shanghai bok choy, cut in half

¼ cup sliced red and green bell peppers

1 cup spinach leaves

1 cup bean sprouts

2 cups steaming rice

Cover the mushrooms with ¾ cup boiling water and allow to sit for 30 minutes. (You may use this mushroom-soaking liquid in making your vegetable stock; see page 66.) With your hands, wring out the mushrooms over the mushroom soaking liquid; cut off and discard the stems. Slice the mushroom caps in half on the bias.

To make the sauce, mix the vegetarian broth with the oyster sauce, sugar, garlic, and ginger in a saucepan, and bring to a boil. Add the cornstarch mixture and boil just until thickened and clear.

Combine the vegetables and the bean curd in a bowl, put the bowl in the top of a steamer containing rapidly boiling water, and steam until just done, about 5 to 7 minutes. Arrange over the steaming white rice; pass the sauce for the diners to help themselves.

Serves 1 or 2 as a complete meal,
3 to 4 as part of a larger meal

Spring Vegetables in Thai Curry Sauce

○

A wonderful lightly creamy, lightly curried seasonal vegetable dish that can hold its own with any main dish on the table. The vegetables selected below are one suggestion among many that work especially well in the spring. Feel free to try different combinations. The vegetables should total about ¾ of a pound to a pound.

⅔ cup of unsweetened coconut milk

⅓ cup of chicken stock

1 cup fresh asparagus, trimmed and cut into 2-inch lengths on a bias

¼ cup sliced bamboo shoots

4 hearts of Shanghai bok choy, cut in half

¼ cup sliced red and green bell peppers

12 snow peas

2 tablespoons peanut oil

2 rounded tablespoons of Yellow Curry Paste (page 16)

4 teaspoons fish sauce

1 tablespoon fresh lime juice

1½ teaspoons sugar

2 teaspoons cornstarch mixed with 2 tablespoons water

Combine the coconut milk and chicken stock in a sauce pan and bring to a boil over high heat. Turn the heat to low and simmer to reduce to ¾ cup of liquid; set aside.

Heat a skillet or wok over high heat. When hot, add the oil. Add the asparagus, bamboo shoots, bok choy, and peppers. Cook tossing until well coated with the oil, about 30 seconds. Add the snow peas and toss for another 15–20 seconds.

Push the vegetables to one side of the pan and add the curry paste. Stir briefly, then add the coconut–chicken stock mixture. Bring to a boil, reduce the heat slightly and allow to simmer for 30 seconds. Add the fish sauce, lime juice, and sugar, and continue to cook, stirring, briefly. Remix the cornstarch and water and add. Cook just until the sauce coats the vegetables, about 20 seconds or so. Turn off the heat. Serve with white rice.

Serves 1 or 2 as a main course, 3 to 4 as part of a larger meal

Braised Napa Cabbage with Chestnuts

○

A simple, comforting, winter Shanghai dish, this is an unusual cold-weather special. It's easy to make and is a wonderful accompaniment to roasts and casseroles.

SAUCE

2 tablespoons sugar

1 tablespoons dark soy sauce

1 tablespoons light soy sauce

¼ cup peanut oil

1 head napa cabbage, about 3 pounds, cut in half lengthwise, and the leaves cut into 2 x 2-inch pieces

8–10 whole chestnuts, peeled

Few drops sesame oil for garnish

Combine the sauce ingredients.

Heat a large skillet or wok over high heat and add the oil. Stir in the cabbage and sauté until it shrinks by almost half (this will take a few minutes).

Add the sauce and cook, stirring, another minute. Add the chestnuts and continue to cook another 30 seconds. Sprinkle with sesame oil and serve.

NOTE: Chestnuts may be peeled more easily by scoring each with two perpendicular slashes and simmering in water to cover for 30 minutes. Allow to cool.

Serves four as part of a larger meal

Bok Choy Flowers and Soy Beans, Stir-Fried with Ham

○

In the spring, various "flowering" bok choys are available at Asian markets, some with yellow flowers, some with white. Either can be stir-fried with the edible soy bean the Japanese call *edamame*, popularly served salted and in the pod in sushi bars. In eastern China, vegetable dishes are typically seasoned, as below, with a kind of hard ham, similar to Virginia's Smithfield, that has been cured in Jinhua, south of Shanghai.

1 pound unpeeled edible soy beans (see Note)

1 cup bok choy flowers with stems (see Note)

1 cup chicken stock

1 teaspoon salt

2 teaspoons sugar

1 tablespoon Shaoxing rice wine

¼ cup peanut or vegetable oil

½ cup sliced scallions

⅓ cup finely minced Virginia ham, such as Smithfield

Few drops sesame oil

Remove and discard the pods from the soybeans, keeping the soybeans handy.

Combine the chicken stock with the salt, sugar, and rice wine, and set aside.

Heat a skillet or wok over high heat and add the peanut oil. When it is hot, add the scallions. Cook, stirring, for 10 seconds, then add the soybeans and bok choy flowers. Sauté briefly until the soybeans and bok choy are well coated with the oil; then add the chicken stock mixture. Cook over high heat 3–4 minutes until most of the liquid is absorbed and the beans are tender. Stir in the ham, sprinkle with the sesame oil, and serve.

NOTE: Soybeans, in the shell, may be purchased blanched and frozen in 1-pound bags in markets that carry Japanese goods. For 2 cups of flowers, it's necessary to purchase up to 2 pounds of flowering bok choy, available in Asian markets, particularly in the spring. Pluck off the flowers along with the small stalks they grow in—each should be about 1½ inches to 2 inches in length. Reserve the rest of the bok choy for another use.

Serves 3 to 4 with rice as part of a larger meal

Stir-Fried Spinach with Pine Nuts

○

There's no greater test of one's ability to stir-fry than to cook fresh spinach so that it's just wilted and soft, but hasn't gone one second beyond that point to where it "breaks" and gives up its juices in an unattractive pool. The secret is initially to toss the spinach rapidly in the pan (a large wok works best) so that it's thoroughly coated with oil. Here the dish is topped with golden pine nuts—a staple of northern China and Korea, where the world's best are said to come from.

1 cup peanut oil

¼ cup pine nuts

1 teaspoon kosher salt

2 teaspoons sugar

2 tablespoons Shaoxing rice wine

1 tablespoon very fine julienne of ginger

1 pound of very fresh spinach, washed and thoroughly dry

Few drops sesame oil

Heat the oil in a small sauce pan over high heat to hot but not smoking. Add the pine nuts, stir, and turn off the heat. Allow to sit for 5 minutes or until they are a light golden brown. Remove the pine nuts to a paper towel to drain, reserving the oil.

Combine the salt, sugar, and rice wine, and set aside.

Heat a large wok, preferably 16 inches or larger, over high heat and add 3–4 tablespoons of the peanut oil. When it is hot, add the ginger, sizzle very briefly in the oil, then add the spinach. Cook, stirring and tossing rapidly, for about 20 seconds as you would a salad, until all the spinach leaves are coated with the oil. Add the seasoning mixture, and continue to toss just until the spinach is beginning to wilt. Remove it from the heat, toss a few more times, and transfer it to a serving plate. Sprinkle with the pine nuts and sesame oil, and serve.

Serves 2 to 4 with rice as part of a larger meal

Sweet and Sour Cabbage

○

A simple Northern Chinese cabbage dish that's tasty even when served at room temperature.

1 small head of cabbage (1½ pounds)

½ cup water

½ cup sugar

1 teaspoon salt or to taste

3 tablespoons red wine vinegar

1 tablespoon dark soy sauce

1½ tablespoons cornstarch

4 tablespoons peanut or vegetable oil

1 tablespoon sesame oil

4 to 6 small chile peppers (optional)

Cut the cabbage in half, remove the core, and cut the leaves into 1½-inch squares. Separate pieces and set aside.

Mix water, sugar, salt, vinegar, soy sauce, and cornstarch, and set aside.

Heat a wok or large skillet over high heat. When hot, add 3 tablespoons of the peanut or vegetable oil. Add the cabbage and stir over high heat until the cabbage is slightly wilted, 4–5 minutes. Remove from the pan.

Reheat the pan and add the remaining tablespoon of peanut oil, the sesame oil, and the dried chiles. When the chiles began to smoke and blacken, restir the sauce mixture (the cornstarch should be well combined), and add the sauce to the pan. Cook, stirring the sauce, and when it thickens and clears, turn off the heat. Toss with the cabbage until well coated. Serve.

Serves 3 to 4 with rice as part of a larger meal

15 FRIED RICE

Traditionally a leftover dish or something of an afterthought at many restaurants, fried rice is a dish we take seriously at Big Bowl. It can and should be a delicious meal-in-a-bowl. It's simple to make, and you're limited only by your imagination.

The good news for home cooks is that fried rice puts leftover rice to its best use. In fact it's important to start with rice that has spent the night in the refrigerator so the granules can be separated easily by hand, and they will sauté separately to a much more pleasing "fried rice" texture. Other ingredients don't have to be leftovers, although they can be.

If you're starting from scratch with raw rice for these recipes, plan on about a 75 percent increase in volume when it cooks—e.g., if 3 cups cooked rice are called for, start with 1¾ cups raw rice. Here are six fried rice dishes we serve at Big Bowl.

Vietnamese Fried Rice

○

This elegant fried rice is a mixture of white long-grain rice (we use Thai jasmine) and a small amount of black glutinous rice, available at Southeast Asian and some Chinese markets. Although any main ingredient can be used—shrimp, chicken, clams, etc.—this recipe yields a wonderfully flavored and attractive side dish for a larger meal.

1 cup black glutinous rice (optional, see directions)

1 teaspoon plus a pinch of salt

2 teaspoons sugar

3 cups cooked long-grain rice (3½ cups if black rice isn't used)

1½ tablespoons fish sauce

1 tablespoon fresh lime juice

4 tablespoons peanut or vegetable oil

¾ cup chopped red onion

2 tablespoon finely minced lemongrass

2 tablespoons chopped roasted peanuts

2 tablespoons ground dried shrimp

2 tablespoons Thai basil leaves, lightly chopped

2 tablespoons finely sliced scallion green

2 tablespoons cilantro leaves

To cook black rice, put 1 cup black rice in a saucepan with water to cover by 1 inch. Bring to a boil over high heat; add a pinch of salt and ½ teaspoon of the sugar. Allow it to boil vigorously and add another cup of water. Allow to boil again and turn the heat to a simmer. Simmer, uncovered, stirring occasionally for about 30 minutes (you may have to add a little more water as it cooks). It should be chewy but soft. Take out ½ cup and reserve the rest for another use (like more fried rice the next day; see Note).

With your hands, break up the white rice as best you can to separate the grains.

Combine the fish sauce, lime juice, and remaining 2 teaspoons sugar; set aside.

Heat a wok or skillet over high heat. When hot, add the oil. When the oil is hot, add the onion and stir until translucent. Add the lemongrass and stir for 5 seconds more. Add the white rice and stir, separating the grains by pressing with the back of the spatula, just until coated with the oil. Add in the black rice, if used, and the remaining 1 teaspoon salt, and continue to stir. Sprinkle in the fish sauce–lime juice mixture, and stir briefly. Then add the peanuts and dried shrimp. Cook, stirring, until piping hot. Stir in the basil, scallion, and cilantro, and remove from the heat.

NOTE: Although you're making more black rice than you need, I find you get better results if you cook at least a cup of this rice at a time.

Serves 4 as part of a larger meal

Hangchow White Fried Rice
with Chinese Sausage and Peas

○

This elegant, colorful dish, easy for the home cook, can be eaten for lunch with a salad or as part of a simple supper.

1 Chinese sweet sausage

3 cups cooked rice

1 tablespoon oyster sauce

1 teaspoon light soy sauce

½ teaspoon sugar

1 tablespoon chicken stock

¼ cup peanut oil

1 egg, lightly beaten

½ cup sliced fresh shiitake or white mushrooms

½ cup sliced scallions (green and white)

1 teaspoon kosher salt

¼ cup frozen peas

1 cup fresh bean sprouts

½ teaspoon sesame oil

½ teaspoon freshly ground black pepper

Heat a saucepan with a little water at the bottom over high heat, put in the sausage, cover, and steam for 5 minutes. Remove and, when cool enough, thinly slice the sausage on the bias.

With your hands, break up the rice into grains.

Mix together the oyster sauce, light soy sauce, sugar, and chicken stock.

Heat a large skillet or wok over high heat. When very hot, add the oil. When the oil is almost smoking, add the egg. Cook rapidly until just set and push to the side of the pan. Add the mushrooms and cook until soft; add the scallions and stir briefly to coat with the oil.

Add the rice and salt to the pan and cook, stirring, over high heat, until the rice is coated with the oil and the ingredients are mixed. Add the oyster sauce mixture and stir until the color is uniform. Add the peas and the sausage, and continue to stir. When the dish is piping hot, add the bean sprouts and immediately pull off the heat, and toss. Sprinkle over the sesame oil and black pepper, and serve.

Serves 2 or 3 as part of a larger meal

Shrimp Fried Rice

○

A great version of a Chinese-American classic. For the shrimp you can substitute beef or chicken.

6 ounces shrimp, shelled, deveined, and cut in half lengthwise

1 teaspoon cornstarch

1 teaspoon sesame oil

3 cups cooked rice, preferably left overnight in the fridge

1 tablespoon oyster sauce

2 teaspoons light soy sauce

2 teaspoons dark soy sauce

1 teaspoon sugar

¼ cup peanut oil

1 egg, lightly beaten

½ cup sliced scallions (green and white)

8 fresh snow peas

½ teaspoon kosher salt

1 cup fresh bean sprouts

½ teaspoon freshly ground black pepper

Mix the shrimp with the cornstarch and sesame oil.

With your hands, break up the rice into grains.

Mix the oyster sauce with the soy sauces and sugar.

Heat a large skillet or wok over high heat. When very hot, add the oil. When the oil is hot, add the egg. Cook rapidly until just set and push to the side of the pan. Add the scallions and snow peas, and stir briefly to coat with the oil. Add the shrimp and cook, stirring to separate the pieces and just until they change color, about 30 seconds.

Add the rice to the pan and cook, stirring, over high heat, mashing the rice with the back of a spatula to separate the grains. When the rice is hot and the ingredients are mixed, add the salt and continue to stir. Stir in the oyster sauce mixture. When the color is even and the dish is piping hot, add the bean sprouts. Immediately remove from the heat and toss. Sprinkle with the black pepper and serve.

Serves 1 or 2 as a complete meal, 3 to 4 as part of a larger meal

Thai Chicken Coconut Curry Rice

○

Throughout the tropical world the combination of rice and coconut milk provides nutrition and great taste. This version is spiced with fresh curry, basil, and lime.

3 cups cooked jasmine rice (should be leftover)

¾ cup canned unsweetened coconut milk

8 ounces boned chicken, cut into ½-inch cubes

2 teaspoons cornstarch

¼ teaspoon salt

1 teaspoon sesame oil

1 cup peanut or vegetable oil

½ cup 1-inch cubes red onion

1 tablespoon julienned fresh red hot chili or sweet pepper

2 heaping tablespoons fresh curry paste (pages 16 and 17)

2 tablespoons chicken stock

¼ cup frozen peas

1½ tablespoons freshly squeezed lime juice mixed with 2 teaspoons sugar

1½ tablespoons fish sauce

1 heaping tablespoon julienned Thai basil leaves

¼ cup coarsely chopped fresh roasted peanuts

With your hands, break up the rice into grains and set aside. Put the coconut milk in a saucepan and, over medium heat, reduce to about ½ cup. Set aside.

Toss the chicken with the cornstarch, salt, and the sesame oil, and set aside.

Heat a small wok or saucepan over medium-high heat and add 1 cup oil. When hot but not smoking, add the chicken, and cook, stirring, until the meat just begins to turn color. Remove to drain; reserve the oil.

Heat a clean wok or skillet to hot and add 2 tablespoons of the reserved oil. Add the onion and pepper, and cook until the onion is translucent. Push the vegetables slightly to the side and add the curry paste to the pan. Cook briefly, stirring, and add the rice; cook, stirring and separating the grains, until the rice and curry paste are well mixed.

Add the chicken stock, ½ teaspoon salt, and the reduced coconut milk. Stir until hot, then stir in the peas and the chicken. When piping hot, add the lime juice–sugar mixture and the fish sauce. Stir in the basil leaves and peanuts, and serve.

Serves 2 as a complete meal, 3 to 4 as part of a larger meal

Tea-Smoked Chicken Fried Rice
with Fresh-Shucked Corn and Peas

○

At Big Bowl we use both smoked duck and chicken for fried rice. Feel free to substitute leftover roast chicken (or even holiday turkey) for the smoked chicken in this recipe.

⅓ cup freshly shucked corn (from about 2 ears)

⅓ cup fresh peas

3 cups cooked rice

2 tablespoons oyster sauce

1 tablespoon light soy sauce

1 teaspoon sugar

4 to 5 tablespoons peanut oil

1 egg, lightly beaten

¾ cup sliced smoked chicken, including skin (page 88)

3 fresh mushrooms, thinly sliced

½ cup scallions (whites)

¼ cup diced bamboo shoots (cut into ¼-inch dice)

½ teaspoon kosher salt

¾ cup fresh bean sprouts

½ teaspoon black pepper

Few drops sesame oil

Blanch the corn and peas in boiling water to cover until just cooked, about 1 minute.

With your hands, break the rice apart into grains.

Mix together the oyster sauce, light soy sauce, and sugar, and set aside.

Heat a large skillet or wok over high heat. When hot, add the oil. When the oil is hot, cook the egg, stirring. When set, push the egg to the side of the pan. Add the chicken and mushrooms, and cook, stirring, until the mushrooms soften. Add the scallion whites and bamboo shoots, and cook, stirring. Add the corn and peas, and continue to cook for another 20 seconds.

Add the rice and salt, and cook until hot, stirring and mashing to break up any clumps. Add the oyster sauce mixture and stir until piping hot. Add the bean sprouts and pepper, and immediately pull off the flame. Continue to stir—the bean sprouts should be crisp—and sprinkle with the sesame oil and serve.

Serves 2 as a complete meal, 3 to 4 as part of a larger meal

Curry Fried Rice
with Mussels and Chinese Sausage

○

The touch of sweet richness provided by the sausage complements the mussels in this dish and fried rice is the best possible use of freshly made Thai curry paste. Clams, shrimp, or other seafood may be substituted for the mussels.

1 Chinese sweet sausage

8 small mussels (or clams), scrubbed and debearded

3 cups cooked rice

1 tablespoon fish sauce

2 teaspoons fresh lime juice

1 teaspoon sugar

2 to 3 tablespoons peanut oil

1 egg, lightly beaten

¼ cup sliced scallion (whites)

1 to 2 fresh red chile peppers, seeded and sliced

½ cup green beans, blanched and cut into ½-inch lengths

¼ cup fresh Yellow Curry Paste (page 16)

1 tablespoon julienned Thai basil leaves

1 cup fresh bean sprouts

½ teaspoon freshly ground black pepper

Warm a saucepan with a little water at the bottom over medium-high heat, put in the sausage and mussels, cover, and steam just until the mussels open. Discard any that don't open. Remove, reserving any liquid, and when cool enough, slice the sausage thinly on the bias, and set the mussels and sausage aside.

With your hands, break up the rice into grains.

Mix together the fish sauce, lime juice, and sugar.

Heat a large skillet or wok over high heat. Add the oil and when very hot, add the egg. Cook rapidly just until set and push to the side of the pan. Add the scallion, chile peppers, and green beans, and sauté briefly. Shove these vegetables aside, add the curry paste, and cook, stirring, for a few seconds, just to release the flavor.

Add the rice to the pan and cook, stirring, over high heat, until the rice is coated with the oil and the ingredients are mixed. Add the mussels, sausage, and any reserved steaming liquid, and continue to stir. Add the fish sauce mixture and the basil, and stir. When the dish is piping hot, add the bean sprouts, immediately pull off the heat, and toss. Sprinkle with the black pepper and serve.

Serves 2 as a complete meal, 3 to 4 as part of a larger meal

INDEX

163

173